Library of the Theological Seminary.

PRINCETON, N. J.

Collection of Puritan Literature.

Division

Section

Number

SCB
11185

5/6

JAMES ARMINIUS.
For Learning, Mildnesse and for Sanctitie
Few ever had with him Equalitie.

The Life and Death
OF
JAMES ARMINIUS,
AND
SIMON EPISCOPIUS.

Professors of Divinity in the University of *Leyden* in *Holland*.

Both of them famous Defenders of the Doctrine of Gods Universal Grace, and Sufferers for it.

Now published in the *English* tongue.

Petrus Bertius

The memory of the just is Blessed, Pro. 10. 7.

LONDON,
Printed by *Tho. Ratcliff* and *Nath. Thompson*, for *Francis Smith*, at the *Elephant* and *Castle* without *Temple-Bar*, 1672.

THE
PREFACE.

Courteous Reader,

THE Title-page of the Book presented here to thy view, does sufficiently inform thee, what in the general thou art to expect therein. The book is so little, and may be read over in so short a time, that it is altogether needless to give a further account of its Contents. A large Preface me thinks would be uncomely, as being unproportionable to the Building: And indeed thou hadst not at all been troubled with any Proem how short soever; If I had not a few words to speak touching my work in this English Narrative. Although I was much perswaded and well assured in my self, that a Work of this kind might be of great advantage to those of my Countrey men, who have ears for no other but their Mother tongue, especially to them who have been abused by the Tongues or Pens of any, that have exposed to obliquy and reproach the venerable names of these two reverend men, which alas! many have done, especially as to Arminius: for the other, I mean Episcopius, has not been so generally taken notice of, and his name was not here so publickly known, till the Doctrine, which both of them contended and suffered for, was more commonly known and received amongst us; Yet was

The Preface.

it far from me to undertake of meer choice this endeavour, being not so well conceited of mine own abilities, as to thrust my self into this Imployment, nor so destitute of work as to need this for securing and keeping my self out of idleness; but by the importunate solicitation of some good men, I was prevailed with, and drawn unto it. The Historie of Dr. Arminius is nothing else but that Elegant Latin Oration, here turned into plain English, which learned Bertius delivered in such an Assembly, where he could not deliver untruths and remain undetected. I have indeed scarce pleased my self in translating so Grammatically and verbatim the Testimonies there produced: Yet have so done, that some might not be displeased, who deem such a translation in such cases to be at least convenient. That which thou hast here touching Episcopius, is taken chiefly out of that excellent and large Preface, prefixed to one of the Volumes of his Works, and written by Stephen Curcellæus of blessed memory. In what I have done in the whole I am not conscious to my self of any unfaithfulness, neither am I unwilling to constitute mine Enemies judges of the performance, in case they be fit to examine, and not resolved to be unrighteous in judgment. Reader, I shall no longer detain thee from the profitable exercise of reading the following Narrative, which God almighty bless to thy use. Farewell.

J. K.

THE ORATION

of Peter Bertius *concerning the life and death of that Reverend and most Famous Man* * *Mr.* James Arminius, *which after his sad funeral, was delivered in a Theological Auditory* * Octob. 22. 1609.

* the Divinity School in the University of Leyden.

Magnificent, Reverend, Most noble, Most learned Auditors,

AS heretofore I have oft experienc'd, how hard and how difficult a thing it is, to speak of Excellent persons in an assembly of Renouned men: So now especially I have thereof a sensible knowledge, it being my task at present to speak in this place concerning that Reverend man Mr. *James Arminius*, Dr. of sacred Theologie, and this after the sad solemnity of his Funeral. For sith that a good man is the rule and measure of things, he therefore, that would describe to others such a person, must be carefull to choose out and offer such things to their view, by which humane life may receive advantage in the study of vertue. Good things that lie in secret, must be brought on the stage and made publick, and those things which either Modesty hath concealed, or Envy diminished, or Calumny defamed, or which others through want of skill have not observed, those things I say, when the curtain's drawn back and a light brought in, must be shown openly, and declared by words, that all may behold what in every one is most praise worthy, and what is fit for their imitation. Whence it comes to pass, that the greater every ones vertue is, the more difficult it is to act the Orotors part in speaking of him: for the greatest Envy keeps company with the greatest Vertue. And sith that a wise man doth nothing without Reason; and it being difficult to explicate and unfold at every turn the principles and causes of particular actions, on which the judgment to be made of every thing does depend; it must needs be very difficult to judge of excellent persons, all whose life is full of diverse examples, for the well instructing of others, how to judge, how also to live. And this also may be added, that he who takes upon him this imployment must very frequently have recourse from the law to a mans life, and from his life to the law: for these need each the other, and as the law gives notice what must be done: so what may be done the life sheweth. Now a wise man hath both these in himself; just after the example of Christ our Lord and Saviour, who first said, *Learn of me*: and of his Apostle who thus admonisheth, *Be ye followers of me, as I am of Christ*. And as heretofore *Polycletus*, not contenting himself that he had written a book, wherein he had noted all things to be observ'd by him that would artificially make the image or statue of a man, did himself afterwrrds make the statue of a man, lest he should seem to prescribe that to others which himself had not observed, and this statue made publick he call'd the Canon or Rule, commanding that the lineaments of art should be fetch'd thence as from a law of direction: So a good man, when he hath admonish'd others what they must doe, does first himself perform, what he prescribes to others. Now it is hard, either to bring all a wise mans actions to their proper rule and law, or in one to find the Examples of all laws. But as for me, who am at this day to speak in this honourable assembly of learned men, concerning the life and death of that Reverend and Incomparable man, Doctor *James Arminius*, not only those difficulties, which I have now mentioned stand in my way, but many others also. My Grief, yet fresh, for the loss of a friend presseth me; the consideration of a sad family, an afflicted wife, nine fatherless children disturbs me; the Lamentation of the University moves me; but I am astonished to think of the Church and Common wealth deprived of a man so greatly usefull. All which things, in a wound so fresh, not yet skinn'd over, may easily put to a loss the most eloquent and the wisest man whosoever he be. To what hath been spoken may be added, That he himself, whilst he liv'd, greatly dislik'd all pompous funeral solemnities: for he knew, that the first step to the veneration and worshiping of Saints was hence, and he deem'd, that it unbecomes us to desire and use such Solemnities, that had such hazards attending on them. But seeing our present condition seems to be such, that we need not in the least to be afraid of this (for alas! hitherto are we come, that henceforth it may seem needfull to use diligent care, rather to bring in devotion, than drive superstition out) And sith that it concerns all men, that examples of vertue being drawn forth should be proposed for all to look upon, I have, according to the custom, through the request of friends, and the Senate willing it, undertaken that difficult task, which I

could

could not refuse without the violation of Christian charity, and the breach of the obligation of that friendship, which I have maintain'd with him from my very youth. Which things being so, I hope there will no reprehender of this my duty be found in this assembly of excellent oratours, in which there is no one but is able more gravely and elegantly to perform this charge, than my self. Notwithstanding, I beseech and most humbly intreat you, Magnificent, Reverend and most learned Auditors, to suffer the things I shall speak to be of credit and account with you.

We have committed to the bosom of the earth the body of that Reverend man, Mr. *James Arminius* (or rather the temple of the holy Ghost) which has been shaken, worn, broken with labours, watchings, conflicts, diseases, troubles. We have committed it, I say, in certain hope of a blessed resurrection, which he himself, whilest he liv'd, believ'd, and unto which he directed all his thoughts and purposes.

The place of his birth was *Oldwater*, a little Town long since made famous by the interflowing river *Isala*, and the pleasantness with the fruitfulness of the adjacent country, and the frugality with the industry of its Inhabitants. He in this Town first saw the Sun in the year 1560. in which year the Conference at *Possiack* in *France* began; in which conference our Deputies pleaded the cause of two thousand one hundred and ninety Churches, that did humbly and earnestly desire of the King, peace and tranquility, and the liberty of professing their faith. This year, this *Oldwater*, as another *Sparta*, gave *Arminius*, as another *Lacon*, to the world: which Town notwithstanding at other times brought forth *John de Oldwater*, *Cornelius Valerius*, and that excellent old man, whom ye here behold, Mr. *Rudolphus Snellius*, the ornament, not onely of his native place, but also of this whole University, and especially of them who are of the Senatorie rank and quality.

Arminius whilest an infant lost his father: His mother, a widow burthened with three children, lived all her life long in a mean estate, but honestly.

There was then in that Town a certain Priest, a man honest, and grave, *Theodore Æmylius* by name, whose memory, by reason of his singular learning and holiness of life, is yet blessed among the living. He, when he had got a tast of a better and more pure doctrin in Religion, determin'd with himself, that he would not once more celebrate the abominable sacrifice of the Mass: therefore he oft changed his place of abode, and lived sometimes at *Paris*, sometimes at *Lovane*, sometimes at *Colen*, sometimes at *Utrecht*. He therefore took care, that this fatherless child, *James Arminius*, so soon as his age was capable of instruction, might be furnished with the first rudiments of the Latin and Greek tongue, and with the principles of true piety and religion. And when he perceiv'd in him some appearances of an excellent disposition to vertue, he oft times exhorted him, that all considerations of earthly things being layd aside and contemned, he would give up himself to follow after God and his conscience. He told him, that the time of mans life here is but short, that there follows a condition after this life, which should be estimated not by outward adversity or prosperity, but

by

by the Eternity of happiness or death. This Exhortation, afterwards confirmed by a diligent reading of the holy Scriptures, and pious meditations, was setled upon his heart: And so he, through the hope of that life, underwent every labour, all hazards, with a glad and chearful mind. But after he had for some years thus liv'd ot *Utrecht*, an unexpected calamity did oppress him, by means of the death of that good old Religious man, which the merciful God did suddenly mitigate; for presently upon his death Mr. *Snellius*, who long before flying the *Spaniards* tyranny, went to *Marpurg*, came as it hapned out of *Hassia* into that Countrey. He therefore carried away with him into *Hassia*, in the year 1575. this his Country-man *Arminius*, now destitute of all humane help and succour. He was scarce set down there, when in the Moneth of *August* the report of his Countreys desolation is brought thither; He hears that the Town was taken by the *Spaniard*; that the Garrison were slain; that the Townsmen were kill'd, and the Town burnt. With this report he was so much stricken at the heart and so greatly troubled, that he spent 14 whole days, in continual weeping and tears: Therefore as one impatient he left *Hassia* and went with speed into *Holland*, being determined either to see the ruines of his Country, or to loose his life.

When he was come thither, he found nothing but where the Town stood, and the ruines of it: and understood that most of its Inhabitants were finally slain, together with his Mother, his Sisters, his Brothers and his Kindred: He therefore returned even on foot out of his own Country, to *Marpurg* in *Hassia*. In the mean while this new Academy was erected and opened by the authority of the moſt Illuſtrious Prince of *Orange*; which as ſoon as he underſtood, he prepar'd for a journey home. He came therefore to *Roterdam*, to which place were come from *Amſterdam* many faithfull Exiles, and moſt of *Old-waters* Inhabitants, that had eſcaped the ſword of a cruel enemy. At that time my Father *Peter Bertius*, was the Paſtor of that Church: but Mr. *John Taffinus* was the Princ's *French* Preacher and Counſellor; both theſe were wonderfully pleaſed with the young mans towardlineſs, readineſs and wit. Now ſeeing it was long before my Father was acquainted with learning (for he was 30. years old before he had any knowledge even of the Latin tongue) he upon requeſt of friends, took the young man very willingly into his houſe. Now it was the purpoſe of friends to ſend him to this new Univerſity; which occaſion my Father thinking not good to neglect, calls me out of *England*, when I was then a Student, applying my ſelf to learning: both of us therefore were ſent together into this School: from that time there has been always between us a very great intimacy, familiarity and friendſhip: But I will not ſpeak of the paſſages of that time. This one thing I will ſay, that our young Scholars endeavour in learning and in the ſtudy of wiſdom, was ſo great, their reverence towards their Teachers ſo great, their zeal and earneſt affection in Religion ſo great, that greater could hardly be: But in our rank *Arminius* was one that excel'd the reſt; if any thing was to be written, if any thing to be ſpoken, *Arminius* was ſought for: If then aroſe any debate in learning that required a *Palæmon*, *Arminius* was conſulted with. I remember when Dr. *Lambert Danæus*, our Profeſſor,

did

did commend him publickly for his natural endowments, and for his proficiency, and for his vertue, and did excite us to enter on the study of Divinity with cheerfulfulness, after his example. Why should I make mention here of his study in Poetry, in which he excel'd? Why should I speak of his study in the Mathematicks, and in the other parts of Philosophie? He toucht nothing of these, which he did not penetrate, he set upon nothing, which he did not happily finish.

Thus we are come to the year 1582. in which year the honourable Senate of *Amsterdam* sent him away to *Geneva*, for his more abundant proficiency in learning. Whither when he was come, he heard that reverend old man, and of blessed memory, Mr. *Theodore Beza* expounding the Epistle to the *Romans*, with the great admiration of all men; for there was in *Beza* beyond other mortals a flexanimous and perswasive eloquence, a prompt and ready utterance, perspicuity of speech, pleasantness of voice, but excellent doctrine in the judgment of all learned men. Him therefore above all others *Arminius* made choice of to imitate and follow; But seeing he could not forthwith procure to himself the favour of some Principal men in this School, and that (to speak the truth) only upon the account of *Ramus*'s Philosophy, which with earnestness he defended publickly, and did also in private teach it to his auditors, he was provok'd to go to *Basil*. Where what great honour was confer'd on the young man, what were the presages and divinings of men of all ranks concerning his growing vertue, they are able to testifie, who were his fellow travellers, and companions in this his peregrination. But he so heard these judgments and acclamations, that he never waxt proud and arrogant, but shewed in very deed, that he was unwilling to endeavour by ambition, but was willing by true vertue to come unto that, whereto he was designed by the goodness of God.

At *Basile* in the harvest Festivals the more learned Students are wont out of the ordinary course, for exercise-sake to teach something in the University, someties publickly. This labour our *Arminius* willingly undertook, for this he was prais'd by that reverend man, Mr. *James Grinaus*, who also oft times honoured his lectures by his Presence. The same man also in publick disputations, if any thing more weighty than ordinary were proposed, or an intricate matter worthy a defender, did occur, was not afraid for honours sake to call our *Arminius*, sitting among a great number of Students, and (that you may know the candor of *Grinaus*) to say. *Let my Hollander answer for me*. At this time *Arminius* was in so great favour and renown for his learning, that when he was about to depart thence for *Geneva*, the Theological faculty would have conferr'd on him, even at the publick charge, the title of Doctor, which he, esteeming it too great a dignity for one of his years, did at that time modestly refuse, and gave them thanks for their grace and favour.

When he was come back to *Geneva*, he found the minds of his friends more pacified towards *Ramus's Philosophy*; also he himself thinking it something meet to abate somewhat of his earnestness, did so order himself, that all might easily perceive, that gentleness conjoyn'd with so great a wit brought no small ornament to his age. There were at the same time in the City the Sons

of

of the chief of our Nobility, most of which now are in eminent and honourable places in our Republick. When some of these were gone into *Italy*, others of them called home, he seeing himself alone, and destitute of all others his companions, excepting one, a man of very great dignity now in *Holland*; he also purposed to go with speed into *Italy*, being inclin'd thereunto especially through the fame of *James Zabarella*, who then at *Padua* professed Philosophy, and was greatly followed. For his sake especially he stayed at *Padua*, when he instructed in Logick some noble *Germans*. But afterwards he took a cursory view of the rest of *Italy*, on which journey he spent not above eight months, and at *Rome* he was never absent from that companion of his, who was to him as another *Achates*; for so it was agreed on before they went from *Geneva*. They us'd the same lodging, the same table, the same bed; they went in and out together; and for the exercise of piety they carried with them the Greek Testament and Hebrew Psalter.

I remember he was wont often to tell, That *Italy* brought to him many commodities and discommodities. Among the commodities he plac'd this especially, That he had seen at *Rome* the mystery of iniquity to be far more filthy and abominable than ever he had conceiv'd it in his mind: for he said, that the things which are told or read concerning the *Roman* Court of *Anti-christ*, are Trifles in comparison of the things which he had seen. Among the discommodities this; That the honourable Senate of *Amsterdam* was then somewhat offended at him for that his *Italian* journey, some in the mean while augmenting their their displeasure, who clearly had
done

done better in suspending their opinions till his return. Hence then an occasion being taken, it was noys'd among the common people, That he had kist the *Popes* pantofle; whom he had never seen but as other spectators did, in a great throng and croud of people. (And indeed that Beast is not wont to give this honour to any but Kings and Princes.) Also, that he was accustom'd to hear the *Jesuites*, when as he never heard them; That he was acquainted with *Bellarmin*, whom he never saw; That he had abjur'd the orthodox Religion, whereas he was ready to contend for it even to the loss of his life.

Now let our Youth that are pious and devoted to the Church learn this from anothers harm, That it is better never to set foot in *Italy*, than with so great an hazard of their repute to know the mysteries of *Antichrist*. Not because it is more dangerous for them to see *Italy*, than neighbouring *Antwerp*, or *Brussels*, or *Brugs*: for in *Italy* there is much more liberty, and in these places more superstition by far. And it is safer to travel throughout all *Italy*, than *Brabant* or *Flanders*: but because it is expedient to take all occasions of evil speaking from the adversary, and all occasions of evil-surmising from those that are unadvised and imprudent. And it is better to prevent an occasion of offence, than to excuse it.

Being come out of *Italy* he stayed at *Geneva*, and some months after being called home he returned to *Amsterdam* to his *Patrons* and *Masters*, furnished, *through the grace of Christ, with a clear testimony* from them of *Geneva, and with a mind very well fitted to do office, if it might please the Lord God to use his ministry,*
for

for his Work in his Church: For these are the very words of Mr. *Beza's* Epistle, the original of which I have in remembrance. At *Amsterdam* he did easily, with grave and prudent men, clear himself as to his *Italian* journey: but indeed the weak brethren went on inveighing against it, and in their assemblings blaming it till he himself began to be heard in the Church, in which as soon as he was beheld, it cannot be spoken, with how much respect men of all ranks flocked together to hear him: For there was in him (as ye know) a certain incredible gravity mixed with gracefull pleasantness. His voice indeed was slender, but sweet, and loud, and piercing, but he had an admirable perswasive faculty. If any thing were to be adorn'd, he so did it, as not to exceed the truth. If he were to teach any thing, he did it with clearness and perspicuity. If he were to dispute any thing, he manag'd the same distinctly. Now the Melody and altering of his voice was so fitted to things, that it seemed to flow from them. And sith he did not use a Rhetorical dress, and the Greeks boxes of pleasant ointment: it was either because his nature did abhor them, or because he judged it unworthy the majesty of Divine things, to use curles, and borrowed ornaments, when as the naked truth is of its self sufficient for its own defence: notwithstanding he so efficaciously perswaded by force and weight of arguments, and by the pithiness of his sentences, and by the authority of Scripture it self, that no man ever heard him, but confess'd, that his discourses much affected him. Some therefore at that time called him the polishing life of truth; others the whetstone and sharpner of wits; others called him the razor shaving off growing

errours

errors, and nothing in Religion, and sacred Theology was thought to savour well, that did not relish with *Arminius*. Also the Pastors and Preachers themselves of that City, men both learned and eloquent, did reverence him for his learning, and ingeniously acknowledge themselves to have been daily very much advantaged by his Sermons. And thus our *Arminius* with spread out sayles, prosperous gales, a full company of rowers, and the good wishes of all that knew him, was carried towards fame and glory, when it pleased God to exercise his servant even with adversity, and to make a tryal of his patience and humbleness by the cross and afflictions. Now 'tis a thing worth the knowing, to understand the beginnings and success hereof.

There was carried about as it chanced in the hands of some pious men a little Book, written by some of the brethren of the Church of *Delf*, against Mr. *Beza*, with this Title. *An answer to some arguments of* Beza *and* Calvin *out of a Treatise concerning predestination on the 9. Chap to the* Romans. This little book was sent over to our *Arminius* by Mr. *Martin Lidyus* of blessed memory, who had been formerly a Pastor in the Church of *Amsterdam*, but then was Professor in the *Friezlanders* new Academy, and by him *Arminius* was requested to undertake the defence of Mr. *Beza* against the brethren of *Delf*. For *Arminius* was verily thought a man very fit for this business by Mr. *Lidyus*, who partly by report, partly by experience knew the quickness of his wit, the sharpness of his judgment, and what a wonderful

B force

force and power he had both in preaching and in disputing. Neither was *Arminius* altogether strange from this design, being one that newly coming out of the School of *Geneva*, carryed about with him in his ears the sound of Mr. *Beza's* lectures and arguments. He therefore betakes himself to the work; But whilst he endeavours a refutation, whilst he weighs the arguments on each side, whilst he confers the Scriptures, whilst he torments and wearys himself, he was overcome by the truth. At first indeed he followed that same opinion which he undertook to oppose, but he afterwards by the guidance of the holy Ghost was carried over to that doctrin, which he constantly asserted even to the end of his life: Which was this; That Gods eternal Decree in predestination, was not to elect or chuse precisely and absolutely some to salvation, whom as yet he had not purposed to create; (which Mr. *Beza* would have) neither was it, precisely and absolutely to elect some to salvation after the decree of their creation and the foresight of their fall, but without an antecedent consideration of Jesus Christ; (which the Delfian brethren held) But it was, To elect to salvation them of the created and fallen, who in time to come would by true obedience of faith answer to God calling them thereunto: Which by learned *Melancthon* and *Nicholaus Hemingius*, and many more divines besides, hath been asserted.

And although such in times past hath been the liberty of our Churches, and even now is in very many places, that in this Argument, in which no
ancient

ancient Synod hath ever determined any thing, any one of the multitude, and a Teacher, might always without offence to any one choose this or that: for to omit others, Dr. *Jo. Holmannus Secundus*, who by the very grave advice of excellent Divines, and especially of the Lords Curators was called forth, after Mr. *Pezelius* and *Mollenius* and others were sollicited in vain, taught it out of this very place: He imbraced (as we know) the opinion of *Hemingius*, and sharply defended it. Notwithstanding there were not those wanting at *Amsterdam*, that in this matter were troublesome to *Arminius*, and that accused him for departing from the common and received opinion in our Churches, but their vehemency and fierceness was suddenly repress'd and appeas'd by the authority of the Senate, and the equanimity and moderation of the brethren; so that he always lived with his Collegues at *Amsterdam* quietly, yea friendly and brotherly, without any cloud of displeasure, or hatred, or envy. And also this man of God was not only naturally dispos'd to candor and gentleness, but also was moreover so formed and fashioned thereto by the holy precepts and Spirit of Christ, that he did quietly bear with him that dissented from him, and did not easily despair of any one, that was but willing to hear Christ speaking in Scriptures: which by his divine moderation and equinimity we all knew, and have by so much the more admired it, by how much the further we, by the testimony of our own conscience, perceive our selves yet to be from these good things.

Now when the University, deprived of her Professors by the death of those famous and excellent men, Dr. *Junius* and Dr. *Luke Trelcatius* the elder, sought for an *Hercules* that might sustain this Orb (which in the mean while that Reverend man Dr. *Francis Gomarus*, being destitute of all his Colleagues, did as another *Atlas* support alone) they by the general vote, and the publick consent of their country, came to *Arminius*, who thinking of nothing less, was taking care for the church of Christ at *Amsterdam* which he had served now fifteen years. But when they of *Amsterdam* profest that they could not be without his endeavours amongst them, because as they said, they had chiefly him, by whom they might oppose the growing monsters of heresies, it cannot be spoken how great then the consternation of good men was. They variously deliberate and advise, no stone is left unturned. The Curatours of our University, *viz.* most noble *Dousa* and *Neostadius*, went themselves in the publick name, together with that most honourable man, *Nicholaus Zeystius* the Syndick of our Common-wealth. To the same end Mr. *Jo. Utembogardus*, Pastor of the Church at the *Hague*, was sent by the most illustrious Prince. and also *Nicholaus Cromhousius* out of the supream Court. All these after a diverse manner did earnestly move and perswade the most prudent Senate of this Common wealth, and the Consistorie of the Pastors and Elders. At length by many labours, intreaties, and also the intercession it self of most illustrious Prince, it was hardly obtain'd, that he he should be dismissed from *Amsterdam* and serve the University. Nevertheless petty Rumours of suspicions, which most commonly are wont to subvert the best endeavours, did withstand him, against which he set the shield of his innocency and candour and learning; Trusting in this, he confidently expected the blessing of God in that which was behind. This matter therefore being heard and debated at the *Hague* before the Lords Curators in the presence of some grave Divines, it was found, *That those suspicions were ill supported, and that there was no cause why any one should have an ill opinion of that faithfull servant of Christ: for they found, that he used the allowed liberty of prophesying in the Church, had taught nothing which was contrary to the Christian religion.* He then first obtained in this University, with the good liking of God and men, the degree of Doctor, which in the year 1603 that reverend man Dr. *Francis Gomarus* conferred on him here in this very place. Thus then *James Arminius* succeeded *Francis Junius*, the Curators so commanding it. And that nothing might be wanting here to his credit and authority by reason of those things that had been given out at *Amsterdam*, it pleased the Ecclesiastical Presbyters to commend him to all godly, honest and learned men, by adorning him at his departure with a very fair testimony which soundeth thus.

The Testimony of the Church *at* Amsterdam.

If the reason it self of equity, in the common society of men, was willing long since to have it establish'd for a law, That they should be judged worthy of a singular good commendation, and more honourable testimony of truth, who had any where very well merited of the common-wealth: they much more are worthy of this honour, who labouring in the word of God, have been for many years Ministers of the holy Gospel with singular fruit and praise in the Church of our Lord Jesus Christ. Wherefore sith that Mr. Dr. *James Arminius*, a Reverend brother in the Lord, hath now requested this same of us, we said, that we must by no means deny it him. Therefore we would by this writing testifie to all and every one, that the very great integrity of both the unblameable life and sound doctrine and manners of the forenamed worthy man, and to us all a most dear companion in the Lord, hath now by long acquaintance been so well perceived and tryed by us, that there is nothing of more account with us than always to enjoy his counsell, labour, familiarity and intimacy, and to maintain that friendship which now for a long time hath been between us. But seeing the most blessed and almighty God seems to have appointed another thing concerning him and us, we have cause of giving very great thanks to the Lord our God for that very great benevolence of his towards us and this our whole Church hitherto, through which it

hath

hath come to pass, that we can with very great delight see and perceive fruits not to be repented of, from the study and labour of the foresaid our very dear fellow-labourer in the Vineyard of Christ, which he hath with us unweariedly and cheerfully undergone, here among ours. We all confess with a most willing heart, that we are in all things indebted to this our dearly beloved brother in the Lord, for his alacrity in continuing with us in the same parts of his function, and for his very ready Councel communicated to us, whensoever we desire it. Wherefore that we may briefly say all in a word (because his very great both piety and probity, and his singular learning, seems after a sort by their proper right to challenge it to themselves) we so commend to all godly, vertuous, and learned men, this honourable Gentleman, and our most reverend brother in Christ, that with greater affection and more heartily we are not able to commend, Dated in our Consistory at *Amsterdam, September* 8th 1603.

    In the name of all,

    John Ursinus Minister of the Divine Word, &c. President of the Consistory.

    John Hallius Preacher at *Amsterdam*.

    John Halsbergius Pastor of the same Church.

Yea and the whole *Classis* gave to him their commendatorie Letters which thus run.

(20)

The Testimony of the Classis of Amsterdam.

To all and every one that shall read or hear this our present Testimony, Salvation and Peace through the only Mediator Christ.

Because the most accomplished and learned man Mr. *James Arminius* hath by the illustrious and for learning most famous Lords Curators of the University of *Leyden*, been called from the holy Ministry (which now for many years he hath discharged with very great commendation in the Church at *Amsterdam*) to the publick profession of sacred Theology, and hath been inaugurated publickly thereunto: we were willing at his departure to commend him to the same (Curators) and to all vertuous men by this our present writing, although but little, and to honour him by our Testimony, as the manner is, We therefore the servants of JesusChrist, together with the Elders of the same *Classis* of *Amsterdam*, do testifie, that the foresaid Mr. Dr. *Arminius* has been now fifteen years a member of our *Classis*, in which time he hath taught with much fruit found Doctrine purely, administred the Sacraments according to the Lords institution, and propagated with great zeal the true and Christian Religion, and by his diligent presence hath always adorned our Classical meeting: also by his prudent Counsel hath with others composed matters hard and of great moment, hath always readily sustained all imposed burthens that respected the Churches Edidification, and hath by honesty and goodness of life

adorned

adorned to this very day his holy calling. In a word, he hath shewed himself such both in his holy Office, and in his manner of life towards all, as becomes a true servant of Christ, that we give to him very great and immortal thanks for his benevolence and humanity towards us, by which he hath embrac'd every one of us. We therefore intreat all and every one, of what order soever they be, to have, acknowledge, embrace and favour the foresaid Mr. Dr. *James Arminius*, as such a one as we have said. Also to affect him with such honour, as he, for his eminent and singular gifts shining in him, is worthy of, and according to their ability to help forward his holy endeavours; for the Glory of Gods name, and the Edification of the School and Church. Unto which end we all his Collegues and fellow-servants do heartily desire for him the manifold grace of the Holy Ghost.

At *Amsterdam*, from our Classical meeting on the Calends of *September*, 1603.

John Halsbergius, President of the Classis.

John Hallius, Preacher at *Amsterdam*.

Scribe of the Classis, & in the name of the Classis.

Have the Brethren honourably and laudably enough testified of *Arminius*? thus then he came into the University. From this time all his Collegues have had experience of him as a most Faithful friend; The Schools as a Senator, Professor, Rector; all the Students as a most gentle Father.

Suddenly after his entrance into the University he found, that the Students of sacred Theology, did entangle themselves in the thickets of questions,

and

and did follow Thorny Theormes and Problemes, the Scriptures being neglected. This evil, after the matter had been communicated to his Collegues, he studied to amend, and did in a great measure effect it, for he brought back the antient, and masculine, and mighty kind of studying, and drew back as much as in him lay the wandring youth to the Fountains of Salvation (those pure and slimeless Fountains) that out of them Religion might be sought for: not that Religion which being satisfied with wrangling debates or bare speculation is gotten to feed the phantasie; but that which breaths out charity, and follows the truth which is after godliness, by which youth learn to fly youthful lusts, and having subdued fleshly allurements, to shun the pollutions of the world, and to do and suffer those things, that make a distinction between a Christian and an Heathen. That saying of our Saviour, *Except your righteousness exceed the righteousness of the Scribes and Pharises, ye shall in no wise enter into the Kingdom of Heaven*: he did repeat often to fix the same upon their memories.

In the mean while the consideration of Christians so miserably divided, and driven asunder one from another, troubled him; he seldom spake of it without tears, never without deep and hearty sighs. He declared, that he wished all the scattered members of Christ might grow together in one body, according to the Lords Commandment. He rightly judged, that the Papal Court sought not the things which are of Christ; but the pleasures, the honours, the

the lucre, the pomp of this present world, and Tyranny over the souls as well as the bodies of men: And therefore that no man could or ought to consult with that Harlot about matters of Salvation, and the establishing of a common peace. He judged, that a great part of others were conscienciously and piously affected; and were not divided not so much through an evil intent and purpose, as through doubtfull ambages or obscurities in which many were driven from peace and concord by ignorance, many by the authority of their Ancestours; many through pertinacy or stiffness in those opinions which either themselves had devised or long defended, many through shame of revoking and retracting their writings, lastly many through prejudice and an ill opinion of their brethren. All which he thought might be remedyed, not by killing one another, but by prayers, and by peaceable and friendly instruction, and by the example of an holy conversation. He therefore both exhorted all to piety, and especially took care of this, that when thornie questions and the huge luggage of vain and empty assertions were removed and taken away, with which the Schools make an huge confused noise; those things might be fetcht only out of the Scriptures which might be usefull to bring them to the belief of necessary things, and to lead a good and blessed Christian life. Which endeaur of his, Satan going about to elude and frustrate endeavoured to perswade the inconsiderate, that these things were done by him to get honour to shew the strength of his wit, to cause

innovations,

(24)

innovations, to maintain contention and wrangling. Some therefore through suspicion, that ill counsellour, moved again old *Camarina*, or were the cause of mischief to themselves; but the Professors themselves and the Colleagues, by the prudent advice of the Curators did quell and quash it at its first shooting up: for credit to which matter I have thought that this *Instrument out of the Acts of the Unoversity* is fit to be produced.

"The Professors of the Theological faculty, when it was related to them; That the *Classis* of *Dort* had laid down among other this Grievance [Seeing there is a rumor that some controversies about the doctrine of the reformed Churches have risen in the Church and University of Leyden, the *Classis* have thought it to be necessary that the Synod deliberate concerning these Controversies, and how they may most safely be composed, that all Schismes and offences which thence may arise, may seasonably be removed, and the union of the reformed Churches to preserved against the calamny of the adversaries] "did, when "the Lords Curators and the Consuls asked, whe- "ther any controversies of this sort were certainly "known unto them, answer unanimously, after "the matter had been first privately among them- "selves examined and weighed, That they wished, "that the Classis of Dort had in this matter, acted "better and more orderly; That they thought "that more things were disputed among the Stu- "dents, than it liked them should be; but that

among

"among themselves, that is, among the Professors of
"the Theological faculty there was no difference which
"may appear to be in the fundamentalls of doctrine:
"Also that they would endeavour that the disputati-
"ons of this sort which arose among the students
"might be lessened. Acted the 10th of *August*, 1605.

James Arminius, Rector of the University *pro tempore*.

   Francis Gomarus.
   Luke Trelcatius, Subscribed.

"The very same day, when the same thing was
"also proposed to D. *John Kuchlinus* Regent of the
"Theological Colledge, he answered; That he
"gave his suffrage to those things that had been said
by the Professors

   Subscribed, *John Kuchlinus* Regent.

And thus indeed these things passed at that time; Afterwards the Senators of the High Court, by the will of the illustrious States at the *Hague*, took cognisance of those things that were reported. What their opinion of the whole matter was, I should now relate, but that I think all here present have the knowledge thereof.

But whilest Chrifts Champion thus wrastles, he was at the length laid on his sick bed by a disease, which by his labours; continual fitting, constant studies, and conflicts incurring without any discharge, he had at the last contracted. Now what wonder is it, if he were moved and troubled at that, which might expose to lose his good name, his salvation and his labours: sith that nothing is of more account

to

(26)

to a good man than his good name; nor to a Christian, than his salvation; nor to a Dr. of Sacred Theology than demonstrations taken out of the Scripture. Oppression, saith *Solomon*, makes a wise man mad. That same brought him grief, his grief brought his disease, and this was the cause of his death. Oh horrible evil and viperous, and raised from the lowest part of Hell! How oft have we heard him privately crying out even with sighing, in the words of the Prophet? *Wo is me my mother, that thou hast born me a man of contention to the whole earth: I have neither lent on usury, nor any hath lent to me on usury, and yet all men curse me.* Notwithstanding he himself recalled himself to the inclosures of reason and tranquility, being always couragious, always patient and gentle towards his brethren, for whose sake he was ready to suffer patiently, or as it were to devour, any reproaches whatsoever from the malevolent, and to forget or concoct them, not with a *Cato's* stomack, but that which was wrought in him by the Spirit of Christ.

But his disease lurking in his bowels brake out especially on the 7th of *Feb.* this year: which at that time so discovered it self, that the Physicians forthwith judged, that there was need of a slow and cautious curation. Now although at the begining of his sickness he could hardly move himself: Notwithstanding when he could, having now and then some ease and respite, he omitted not the labours of his lectures and vocation, nor was he wanting to his cause when need was. Therefore again and again, being called,

he

he with speed went to the *Hague*, and there publish'd a famous profession of his faith before many witnesses, and after that last friendly conference he with this one thing after God and the testimony of his own conscience comforted himself, that in a common assembly of all *Holland* he was patiently heard by his most gentle Masters, to whose prudence he attributed so much, that if he should dye, he did hope, that there would not be those wanting that would defend by the patronage of their wisdom and favour the equity of that cause, which they once heard debated. Being carryed home from the *Hague*, he had scarce set himself to that which his masters commanded, *viz*. To write out that exactly which he had proposed in the friendly conference, but the force of disease again assaulted him by so much the more vehemently, by how much the more it had increased by delay and the weakness of his strength. Therefore being pressed with his disease, he by letters written to the illustrious States modestly excused himself, that he could not at the day appointed obey their will: saying, *That by sickness he was forc't to keep his bed; that he had written a great part, which God so willing it, he was now compell'd to break off from. That he had been at another time heard, and that the whole matter was then exhibited in writing; that that might be as much as necessity required: Notwithstanding if they should at all desire those same things he had written that he would take care, that they should have them either full and perfect, if he by the grace of Christ should be restored, or abrupt and broken, if he should die. Moreover tha*

he

he was so far from doubting any whit of that confession he had published, that on the contrary he did stedfastly judge, that it agreed in all things with the holy Scriptures: Therefore that he did persist therein, That he was ready at that very moment to appear with that same belief before the tribunall of Iesus Christ the Son of God, the Judge of the quick and dead.

In the mean while the force of his disease daily increased, whilst the most famous and most expert Physicians, Dr. *Pavius*, Dr. *Sebastian Egbert*, Dr. *Henry Sael*, Dr. *Reener Bont*, resisted it as much as was possible by Art and Industry, and pleasingly allured natures forces, but in vain; for the untamed obstinacy of the disease scorned art it self; For it was deeper planted than to be plucked up; it stirred up daily new Symptomes, Fevers, the cough, the extension of the hypoconders, difficulty of fetching of breath, oppression after meat, troublesome sleeps, an atrophie, the gout, and gave to him no intermission of rest: Afterwards came the Iliac passion, and the Colick, with an obstruction of the left optick nerve, and an obfuscation or dimness of the same eye; In the mean while calumny was as cruel, and abated nothing of its accustomed fierceness; of which I shall here mention, a cruel unworthy and abominable instance, which is fit to be recorded for after ages: When that dimness of one of his eyes was known, there were some that durst account this among those punishments, which God threatens to his enemies, and wicked contemners of his name, and did affirm even from this punishment, that he was

very

very wicked beyond others. And that there might not be wanting a pretext and colour to this so filthy and cruel a deed, the sacred Books are consulted with, which a Christian may not approach without reverence and prayer. A place is found in the Prophet *Zechary* concerning the consumption of the eyes and the whole body, sounding thus. *And this shall be the plague wherewith the Lord will smite all the people, that have fought against Jerusalem: their flesh shall consume away, while they stand upon their feet; and their eyes shall consume away in their holes, and their tongue shall consume away in their mouth,* Zech. 14. 12. And another place; *Wo to the Idol shepheard that leaveth the flock: the sword shall be upon his arm, and upon his right eye: His arm shall be clean dried up, and his right eye shall be utterly darkened.* Chap. 11. 7.

This place was wrested against this holy servant of Christ, who indeed was afflicted in body, but in his soul always happy, but now even most happy and blessed. I tremble at the remembrance of so enormous, and detestable, and ungodly deed. Who, art thou, oh man, that condemnest thy brother, for whom Christ shed his blood? What dost thou revile that servant of God with oracles fetched as it were from heaven itself, whom they that shall come after us, and shall not be ungratefull, will acknowledge to have exceeding well deserved of the whole Church of Christ? Why dost thou take unjustly to thy self a power of condemning thy brother, whom the Lord hath commanded thee to love. Hear him: *Neither this man hath sinned, nor his parents, but these things*

C

are

are done, that the works of God may be made manifest. Hear him again; *Judge not, that ye be not judged.* Hear the Apostle; *It is with me a very small thing, that I should be judged of you, or of mans judgment. He that judgeth me is the Lord; Therefore judge nothing before the time, untill the Lord come, who both will bring to light the hidden things of darkness, and will make manifest the counsels of the heart: And then shall every man have praise of God.* Art thou so assured of what shall happen to thy self, as to know for certain, that thou thy self shalt not be tormented with more bitter pain and dolour? And yet 'twas not his right eye that was amiss; neither was it blindness, but only a dimness, and his arm was not dried up, but swelled. His tongue truly even to the last moment of his life readily discharged its office. Thus things above, things below, things on the right hand, things on the left, things divine, things humane, wait together on these wretched Hierophants [Expounders of divine mysteries] to serve them when they will.

There were somes who playing on his name, devised, *Vani orbis amicus*: [*i. e.* A friend of the vain world.] as if impiety was not sometime bold to do the same on the sacred name of Christ. Go your wayes for beetles, the unprofitable things of the world; What will ye not attempt to do on the servant who have not spared God himself and the Lord of life? But I return to that which I made digression from: He although tired with all these evils, yet notwithstanding kept a stedfast courage and quiet
mind

mind. He therefore never abated any thing of the pleasantness, and comely gracefulness, and accustomed cheerfulness of his countenance, and candor of heart, his most ardent prayers ascending to God for himself and the concord of the church. How frequent, how fervent, in his sickness were his ejaculations to Jesus Christ? What joyes did he promise himself? With what perseverance of faith did he expect his last day in the world? If the brethren did compose themselves to prayers, and he himself was hindred by pain, he now and then desired them to stay till he should come to himself, that he might together with them perform this brotherly office.

These few forms of prayers among many more were noted.

OH great Shepheard of the sheep, who by the blood of the everlasting covenant wast brought again from the dead, Oh! Lord and Saviour Jesus, be present with me thy weak and afflicted sheep. Oh Lord Jesus the faithfull and mercifull High priest, who wast willing to be tempted in all things like unto us, but without sin; that thou learning by experience it self, how hard it is to obey God in sufferings, mightest have compassion on us in our infirmities; have pity on me, and succour me thy servant, who am sick an pressed with many afflictions. Oh God of my salvation! make my soul fit for thine heavenly kingdom, & my body for the resurrection.

Now when upon the increasing of his disease he was admonished by the Physicians, that by reason of

the

the doubtfullness of his life, he would set his house in order, and that if any thing were to be given in charge by his last will and testament, he would take care to do it; he then composed himself for death, with such great quietness of mind, that friends standing by, who had observed the whole manner of his life, admired at his so great and so heroick moderation in the last act, and they took from him the last example of dying blessedly, of whom long before they had learned many things for the well ordering of their lives; He then perceiving that the time of his dissolution was at hand, and not being ignorant of the Devils stratagems, took speciall care, when he made his will, to give a brief Account of his designs and of his life. This, because it contains the duty of a faithfull Teacher, I shall recite for an Example and for a Testimony.

Out of his will or Testament.

BEfore all things I commend my soul, when it shall depart out of its body, into the hands of God its Creator and faithfull Saviour, before whom I witness that I have with a good conscience, singly and sincerely walked in my charge and calling: taking heed with much solicitousness and carefulness, not to propose or teach any thing, which I had not found by a diligent search out of the holy Scriptures, to agree exactly with the same Scriptures; and that I have taught those things which might conduce to the propagation and amplification of the truth, the Christian religion, the true worship of God, common piety, and holy conversation among men; Lastly, to tranquility agreeing to the Christian profession and peace according to the word of God, excluding from among these Papacy, with which no verity of faith, no bond of piety and Christian peace can be kept.

These things being thus finished, some days were spent in the invocation of Christ, and in thanksgiving and the meditation of a better life; In which time Mr. *Jo. Utenbogardus* and Mr. *Hadrian Borrius* did more frequently visit him then others did; Both of them were his old and most faithfull friends; But Mr. *Borrius* was even always present in the daily performance of prayer with his sick friend.

Now at length on the 19th of *October*, about noon, this faithfull servant of God, being discharged of his
warfare,

warfare, having finished his course, fought the good fight, kept the faith, did render his soul now weary of cares, now glutted with the miseries of this world, now defiring deliverance, now having a fore-taft of the joys of the Saints, now feeing Chrift his God and redeemer, did I say, with his eyes lifted up to heaven, render quietly among the holy prayers of them that were prefent, his foul to God the Father his creator, to the Son his redeemer, to the Holy Ghoft his fanctifier, all crying out, *Let me dye the death of the righteous.*

Thus even this our Sun did fet, thus that juft man dyed of whom this world was not worthy; thus the father of fo many prophets was taken away; thus *James Arminius* by the charet of Ifrael and horfemen thereof was carryed from us into heaven and now is free and delivered from miferyes, hath the crown fought for by fo many labours, by fo great holinefs, and enjoys the heavenly Jerufalem, in the great affembly of many thoufands of Angels, and the Church of the firftborn that are written in heaven, and he fees the Judge of all, and the Spirit of juft men made perfect, and Jefus the mediator of the new Teftament, and the blood of fprinkling fpeaking better then that of *Abel*; But he expecteth that day, in which God will make his dead body, which we have laid in the earth, to be conformable to the glorious body of his Son, according to the power whereby he is able to fubdue all things to himfelf.

But we fo long as it pleafes God fhall be toffed with thefe waves, till he, having at fometime compaffion on us also, shall call us, every one in his own order, out of this miry clay into heavenly joys; keeping in the mean while in the church of the saints the blessed memory of Mr. *James Arminius*, with this Elogy.

That he was a Hollander, whom they that knew him, could not sufficiently esteem; Whom they that esteemed him not, did never sufficiently know.

Finally, most worthy Auditors, being desirous to exhort you to the Churches amiable concord, I shall use no other than the words of the Apostle *John*. *Beloved, let us love one another, because love is of God. And whosoever loveth his brother, is born of God, and knoweth God. He that loveth not, knoweth not God; for God is love.*

FINIS.

SIMON EPISCOPIUS.
This Pictur's Substance was a Matchlesse wight
In Learning, boldnesse and a life Upright.

A short and Compendious History of *Simon Episcopius*. Professor of Divinity in the University of LEYDEN in HOLLAND.

Candid Reader,

THat in a very great part, which learned *Bertius* in the preceding Oration, hath justly premised touching the difficulty of his task and Province, who was to describe so excellent a man as Reverend *Arminius*, may be as justly (to say no more) taken up by him that undertakes a description of *Episcopius*, a man well nigh incomparable in all things commendable in a man, in a Christian, in a Minister of the Gospel of Christ.

It's one of *Amsterdams* chiefest Ornaments, and deserves to be recorded with letters of Gold in the memorials of that famous City; that *Simon Episcopius* in the year 1583. was born there.

His Parents, *Egbert* and *Gertrude*, are worthy remembrance, not only for their pious Offspring,

I mean their eldest son *Rembert*, also *John*, but especially the youngest, our *Simon*; (for their other children, four sons and three daughters, all died in their youth or infancy) but also for their own piety, being then zealous professors of the truth, when extream dangers closely attended on every side those that followed her; *Simon Episcopius*, that renowned Person of whom we are now to speak, brought with him into the world many rare natural Endowments, which afterwards by good education and much industry were greatly improved, and were in his conversation choicely imployed to the end of his days. *Rembert*, his eldest brother, soon espying in him grounds of hope as to his usefulness in the best of imployments; did earnestly solicite his Parents to denote him wholly to learning; His Parents, notwithstanding their Estate, was insufficient (by reason of their numerous offspring) to yield him at his studies a competent maintenance; yet, having assistance freely and privately, offered by *Cornelius Benning*, a man of Consular dignity, were perswaded to dedicate their *Simon* to the study of learning. He therefore was committed, as soon as possible, to the care and discipline of *Peter Uekeman*, a Schoolmaster at that time famous; under whose manuduction he in so little time made so great a progress in Latin and Greek, that he was commended by diverse great men to the honourable Senate of *Amsterdam*, which took and received him into the number of their Scholars, when his parents by the advice of Mr. *John Kuchlinus* and Mr. *James*

Arminius

Arminius, and by their perswasion, gave their consent; for at the first they were somewhat averse thereto. When he had at *Amsterdam* run out his course there in the Grammar school, the Curatours of the School did, in the year 1600, declare him by Solemn sentence meet and worthy to be promoted to the University, that he might there apply himself to more high and manly studies: He was therefore sent away to the University of *Leyden*, into the Colledge of the illustrious States of *Holland* and *West-friezland*; in which Colledge was then President that most learned man, *John Kuchlinus*, who when he was minister at *Amsterdam*, had contracted a firm and intimate friendship with the father of our *Episcopius*. This hopeful Plant had not been long in the Academical nursery, but he lost his most loving and beloved Parents; for *Anno* 1602 his father dyed, in the next year his Mother. He though much afflicted with this adversity; yet being thoughtfull, and desirous of his transplanting into some place of usefulness to the Church of God, neglects not the present opportunity of furnishing himself with things convenient and necessary thereunto. Wherefore having sukt in as much knowledge, as was needfull, of the liberal Arts, he extends his endeavours for getting acquaintance with the secrets of Philosophy; In which having spent about three years, he applyed himself most seriously to the studys of Divinity, and with much diligence laboured therein; yet so as to have now and then a recourse to Phylosophy. At length, the Statutes of

his

his Colledge, and his own private affairs requiring it, he fought the title of a Mr. of Arts, and was, being after a severe examination judged worthy, adorned therewith publickly, in the year 1606, by Dr. *Rodolphus Snellius*, that most renowned Professor of the Mathematicks there. After this he purposeth and resolves to give himself wholy to the study of Divinity onely, in which he had already made a considerable progress. And seeing he could not accomplish his earnest desire of visiting forreign Universities, he continued yet two years and above at *Leyden*, where he was a diligent hearer of the Divinity Professors, namely, *Francis Gomarus*, *Luke Trelcatius*, *James Arminius*; and was so diligent and industrious in disputations, and exercitatory Sermons, that he left far behind him most of his equals for age and standing, and was thought worthy to be called to the Ministry. But seeing afterwards, especially after the death of Dr. *Trelcatius*, that unhappy discension about Predestination, which afterwards gave a disturbance to all *Holland*, did not onely secretly glow between the two remaining Professors, but also at length break forth openly; and seeing our *Episcopius* shewed himself more addicted to the opinion of *Arminius*, he found therefore the Pastors, who were of the other party, to be so disaffected towards him, that they, when the honourable Consuls of *Amsterdam*, who had knowledge of his singular learning and good conversation, were desirous of promoting him to the office of a preacher, did by delays, and other

their

their subtle devices, frustrate and elude the good design of the Consuls. *Episcopius* therefore in the year 1609, in which year *Arminius* dyed, left *Leyden* and went to *Franeker*, the *Friezlanders* University, whither he was drawn especially by the fame of *Jo. Drusius*, Professor there of the Hebrew tongue. Here *Sibrandus Lubbertus*, the Professor of this University, took great offence at our *Episcopius*, who was somewhat too hot and fervent in Theological disputations, as young men of prompt and ready wits are wont to be. He therefore a few moneths after departed thence, and went into *France*, where in a short time he got so great acquaintance with the *French* tongue, that he was able not onely to understand it, but also to speak *French* readily and purely. In the year 1610 he returned home, and found the Ministers of *Amsterdam* no better affected towards him than before. But his vertue and learning, which could be no longer hid, and which were commended by clear and notable testimonies from the Churches and Universities where he lived, break thorow at length all obstacles, and so, that he was, with the consent of the Classis, called by the honourable Senate of *Rotterdam* to the Pastoral office at *Bleyswyck*, an hamlet belonging to their jurisdiction.

After the death of *Arminius*, they of Calvins perswasion, whose notions of God, reprobating absolutely the greatest part of the world, to make known his power in making his creatures miserable, had framed and disposed to fierceness, begin to endeavour

deavour the ejection of them out of their places who adher'd to *Arminius*; hereupon these perceiving the designs that were against them, did exhibite to the most illustrious States of *Holland* and *West-friez-land* a certain Remonstrance (whence they were afterwards called Remonstrants, as their adversaries were called Contra-Remonstrants, from a paper they had written in opposition, and intituled, A Contra-Remonstrance) in which Remonstrance after they had declared their judgement comprehended in five heads or Articles, they humbly petition, that they in that belief and perswasion might be protected from the violence and force of their Adversaries that much threatned them. Afterwards in the year 1611 was that famous Conference at the *Hague*, where by the appointment, and in the presence of the States of *Holland* and *West-Friezland*, Six Remonstrant, and as many Contra-Remonstrant Pastors conferred together about the things now in controversy. For the determining of these Controversies, the Remonstrants then declared themselves for mutual forbearance, but their adversaries were for a Synodal Decision, as being no way doubtfull of out-voting them, in case the Remonstrants were admitted members of the Synod, which indeed their adversaries denyed them, when they had gotten a Synod, and the arm of flesh on their side.

But the illustrious States of *Holland* and *West-Friezland*, knowing well, that onely the oppression of the contrary party was sought after, and that the controversie was obscure and difficult, made a decree, that both parties should live together in brotherly communion, &c. which decree had preserved them in peace, if might had not then overcome right, in casting those peaceable Governours out of their places, and substituting those in their rooms who would be ready to doe what the Contra-remonstrants would have.

But we must return to our *Episcopius*, who was one of the six Remonstrants that managed the Conference at the *Hague*, whereas on a famous Theater he made manifest his great abilities, both natural and acquired, and gave all men occasion to conclude, that his knowledge and skill in the holy Scriptures, and in Theological disputations, was not ordinary. After this, the fame of his learning and eloquence spreading in the United Provinces far abroad, he was solicited by diverse eminent Cities, chiefly *Utrecht* to be their Preacher; but seeing they of *Bleyswyck* would by no means be induced to give their consent for his departure, he therefore continued in the exercise of his ministry among them. But at length in the year 1612, when he was about 29 years old, he was called by the Curators of the University of *Leyden*, to the Professorship of Divinity there, in the place of *Francis Gomarus*, who voluntarily had deserted it. Now although the modesty of this worthy man *Episcopius*, was so great, that he judged himself unmeet for a work so difficult in such difficult times; yet suffered he himself to be prevailed with, and overcome by the judgment of others concerning him,

him; and especially by the authority and exhortation of some very great men in the Common-wealth and Church to accept it. In this honourable place, worthy a man so learned and venerable, he lived friendly and peaceably with Dr. *Jo. Polyander*, his Colleague, though of an opinion differing from his in the controversy of predestination; and most painfully laboured in his Office, as even to us is apparent from his Commentaries on some parts of the holy Scriptures, then composed, and his disputations there, which since his death have been exposed to publick view. But his Cares were so many and great, that they far surmounted all his other labours and did much exceed them; For at this time the Controversie about Predestination had swelled over the Academical banks, and had filled the pulpits, whence (as usually) it spread as an inundation among the common people, threatning a devastation of the Churches unity, and to the Common-wealth no less then ruine: For the governours themselves, who were to have kept the peace, were divided among themselves, designing variously for their several parties. In this evil day and contentious time, good *Episcopius*, a man greatly desirous of peace, a manstudious, laborious and solicitous for the good of others, became a man of sorrows, and acquainted with griefs. Now to give a few instances of this mans sufferings, may not onely be serviceable to his commendation, they being the tryal and an evident proof of his sincerity, and that which brought to light his Christian fortitude and patience, wherein he greatly ex-

they may expect, who are of the first in discovering errors, that have been long and more generally embraced for truths, and for such, which men have much gloryed in, as a treasure more peculiar to themselves than others; and also to let us know what are the usual effects of blind zeal in matters of religion, which will appear to be the worst of Guides, leading men to most injurious, inhumane and barbarous practices.

We will begin with that which happened at *Amsterdam*, in the second year of his Professorship; The story in brief in this, *Episcopius* being at a church in *Amsterdam* and (as they commonly speak) standing as a witness with others at the baptizing of his brother *Johns* Daughter, *Caspar Heydan*, who then did officiate, asked him and the other witnesses, *whether they did confess that to be the true* and perfect *doctrine of salvation, which was contained in the old and new Testament, and in the Apostles* Creed, and *which was taught in that church*, to wit, of *Amsterdam*; adding moreover these words: What say ye to these things? *Episcopius*, the chief among them, answered; That he did account whatsoever was taught there according to the word of God, and the Apostles Creed, to be the true and saving doctrine, as the words of the usual form, out of which the interrogation is made, do intend; Which answer, though mild and modest, so moved the spleen of Mr. *Heydan*, that with contempt he called him Young-man, and upbraided him

D

as one very audacious and presumptuous in daring to speak so in the Church of God. To which *Episcopius* again replyed, saying; That he would depart f the Preachers would not admit that limitation, comprehended in the form of Baptism, where after mention made of the old and new Testament, and the Apostles Creed, these words are added, and conseqently is taught in the Christian Church. But when *Heydan* had the second time upbraided him with audaciousness, and *Episcopius* made no further reply, he at length christened the Child. And when *Episcopius* was going out, he was reproachfully handled, and called a seditious man, and a disturber of the Church, by some of the baser sort, whom *Heydans* words had excited to such opprobrious speeches; and when he was gone out of the Church, he hardly escap'd beating or stoning, to which some instigated the youth that were then present. But God out of his fatherly care protecting him, and restraining the fury of those wicked men, brought him at length to his friends in safety.

Not long after this it happened in the same City, That a certain Black smith, seeing *Episcopius* passing by his shop, run out with a bar of Iron that he was forging on his anvil, and called him *Arminian*, and a disturber of the Church; and so pursued him, as one having a mind to murther him, which danger he escap'd by flight and the assistance of others, that hindered and restrained this villanous Zealot.

Now if we should here insert a short but sad story of some Contra-remonstrants Plunderers, we should not go far out of our way, nor much digress because *Arminianisme* (so called) was the occasion, and *Rembert*, the brother of our *Episcopius* was the person pillaged, and that in the time we have now under consideration. The story thus runs ; There was in the year 1617, and on the 19th of *February*, a false rumour raised and spread abroad, that some Remonstrants were met together to hear a Sermon in the house of Mr. *Rembert Episcopius*, who in *Amsterdam* was well known to be much addicted to the Remonstrants opinions, and was for that cause much hated by the vulgar sort, Upon this report many hundreds of vile persons run thither, who first breaking the windows with stones, then with a bar breaking up the gate, enter the house in an hostile manner, and as a Company of Robbers, when they had drank up or spilled the wine and beer in the Cellar, they search and sack the house, opening forcibly above 12 chests, carrying away what was portable, for they stole thence a bag of money, wearing clothes, linnen, pictures, books, houshold-stuff, plate, &c. and what they could not carry away tore and broke, leaving nothing there whole and untouch'd, When they had emptyed the house, they begin to demolish it and make it an heap of rubbish, which they had done, if the coming of the Magistrate had not hindered them. The Gentleman and his wife escap'd their fury; she by flying to a neighbours house; he by hiding himself on the top of his own house, whither he got by a ladder that he drew up after him. His loss was estimated

(12)

to be above six thousand florans. And if he had not had some space (while those religious Felons were breaking open his doors) for the casting of his money and some part of his better houshold-stuff into a neighbours house, he had in that one day been well nigh spoyled of a good estate, and reduced to poverty, The other brother Mr. *Jo. Episcopius*, being also of the Remonstrant perswasion, though he was not pillaged as his brother, yet was he often and much reproached by the dregs of the people, a sort of malignant Zealots But to return now to our *Episcopius*, who was a sufferer in his Relations, and Christian Associates, and met with many great personal afflictions, especially at the time of the Dort Synod, and afterwards, of which we will here take a Superficial and cursory view.

In the year 1618 began the Synod of Dort, which how unjustly it carryed it self towards the Remonstrants, the Acts and History thereof, long since published; do, saith *Curcellæus*, abundantly testify. We will briefly mention here a few things that more nearly touch our *Episcopius*; Although from that which happened not long before the convening of this Synod; namely the violent ejecting of those Magistrates that favoured mutual forbearance, it was not hard to conjecture, that no good issue would attend this Synodical meeting; yet notwithstanding our *Episcopius*, being invited to it by the Letters of the Illustrious States of *Holland*, and to sit there with the other professors of the *United Provinces*, did with some other Remonstrant Preachers

ers make his appearance at *Dort* soon after the beginning of the Synod; But the Synod, which was the adverse Party, and which shamefully took to themselves a power of judging in their own cause, permitted neither him, nor any other Remonstrants to be present in their assembly, but as cited persons, appearing at the Synods tribunal, and submitting to the authority of the Synod, as having power to order them, when to speak, when to hold their peace; and also at length, by majority of voices, to judge and censure them; Which how far from all equity it was, let all judge that have eyes to see, and are impartial. The Remonstrants notwithstanding, lest they should seem wanting to a good cause, did yield to a necessity, and with a great and undaunted courage entred the Synod, and there *Episcopius* with great grace and Oratorial gesture (and as our learned *Hales* expresseth it) recited that excellent Oration, which is to be found in the Acts of the Synod, and in the second volume of his works. After this, when the Remonstrants declared, that they were ready to confer with the Synod, the Ecclesiastical President in the name of the Synod answered, That they by an authority granted to them from the *States General*, were come together, not to confer with them, but to judge them; Notwithstanding this, yet the Remonstrants, having protested, that they could not acknowledge that Synod as a lawfull Judge in the present controversy, because the greatest part of it consisted of their professed adversaries, who had already condemned them, and seperated

from

from them, did addrefs themfelves *freely to propound, explain and confirm their fentence or judgment, before the Synod, fo far as they could and did judge neceffary*; aud fo to do, they were not onely exprefly permitted, but alfo injoyned, by the Deputies of the *States-General* in their Citatory Letters. But when the Synod would again circumfcribe that liberty by thefe limits, to wit, that they fhould propound, explain and confirm their fentence or judgment, *as far as the Synod fhould judge might be fufficient and ought to be*; then could not the Remonftrants fatisfy their confciences to fubmit to fuch uneqaal and unrighteous conditions, by which they fhould betray their caufe, and fo they were at length caft out of the Synod, as perfons unworthy for the Synod any longer to treat withall.

Concerning the manner of their ejection I fhall here adde fomething out of the letters fent from Dort to Sir *Dudly Charleton*, at that time Lord Embaffadour from *K. James* to the *States-General*, and written by Doctor *Belcanqual*, a member of the Synod, and one of the Englifh Colledge there, and of a different perfwafion to the Remonftrants, and by our own renowned Countrey-man Mr. *Hales*, then Chaplain to the faid Embaffadour, but for a time refident at Dort, to obferve the Synods proceedings there; The letters may be found in *Hales* his Golden Remains: When the voices faith (*Belcanqual*) onely of the forreign Divines were asked (who are not above a third part of the Synod) then were the Remonftrants called in, and difmift with fuch such a powdering speech, as I doubt not but that your Lordship hath heard with grief enough. I protest (saith he) I am much afflicted, when I think of it; For if the Remonstrants should write, that the President pronounced a sentence, which was not the sentence of the Synod, they should not lie. The Civil Lawyers and Canon of *France*, who write much about the formalities omitted in the Councel of *Trent*, are exceptions of less moment then these; So neither was there above a third part of the voices asked, *ex quibus sententia fieri nequit*. Neither was the sentence conceived in writ, and approved by the Synod; And the bitter words of the sentence were not the words of ony of the suffrages, unless that some of them were spoken by one man onely. So far he; There are saith (Mr. *Hales*) some exceptions taken by the Deputies themselves against Mr. *President* his rough handling the Remonstrants at their dismission. The next day in the morning there was a private Session, where a repetition was made of the last Synodical Acts, but when they came to the Act of the Remonstrants dismission *Ludovicus Crosius* of *Breme* signifyed, that he perceived, that Mr. *President* in that business had been *paulo commotior*, [somewhat too passionate] and had let slip *Verba quædam acerba* [some bitter words] which might well have been spared; That in so great an act as that was, a little more advise and consideration might have been used, That the Synod ought to have been consulted with, and a form of dismission conceived and approved of by all,

D 4 which

which should in the name of the Synod have been pronounced and registred, whereas now the Synod stands indicted of all the unnecessary roughness which then was practised. So far our *Hales*.

After the dismission of the Remonstrants, the Synod prepared to judge them out of their Writings. But they in the mean time, whilest the Synod was thus occupied, did privately, by the command of the *States Deputies*, compose for the confirmation of their doctrine, those accurate Writings, which together with the Synodal Acts were published a little after, and deservedly obtained the approbation of very many of the most learned men in *Europe*; One of chief authority when he had seen them, said, That the *Dort* Synod had condemned the Remonstrants; but they by their Writings had triumphed over the Synod.

And indeed one substantial argument is better than a thousand Synodal suffrages. The chiefest part of these Writings ought to be ascribed to the indefatigable industry of our *Episcopius*. That nervous Dissertation touching Reprobation had for its Author, that learned and reverend father Mr. *Charles Niellius*, a preacher at *Amsterdam*. To his memory we are indebted not onely for that piece, but for other things also in that volume; and debtours we are to all the rest of them for that share of their labour we have in those Excellent Writings.

At length the Synodical Sentence against the Remonstrants was pronounced, by which they are condemned as men of a corrupt Religion and deposed and put out of Office.

The

(17)

The hard usage of the Remonstrants is not much to be wondered at, the Synods temper being considered; For although there was much candour in some of the forreign Divines, especially our *English*, yet there was much want of it in the Provincials. Not to speak any thing of the unworthy usage which some of the forreign Divines, experienced in the Synod, & particularly they of *Breme*, who were upon the point of leaving the Synod, by reason of offences there given them; I shall onely in a word discover their ill disposition towards the Remonstrants: Prejudice prevailed much among the *Dutch* Contra-remonstrants; They are (saith *Belcanqual* in his letter of *April* 17) so eager to kill the Remonstrants, that they would make their words to have that sense which no Grammar could find in them; We have given a remarkable Instance of the *Presidents* good nature and manners. And as for *Gomarus*, the then visible head of the Fatalists, of what a froward and turbulent Spirit he was, I am even loth to express in the words of *Belcanqual*, who thus writes to the Embassador; If the Synod (saith he) had wanted but two men, I mean *Sibrandus Lubbertus* [one of the principal Contra-remonstrant leaders] and *Gomarus*, we had wanted a great deal of contention, which I fear will not forsake the Synod as long as they are in it; They have their fits of madness by course; The last fit before this came to *Gomarus* his turn, and this day *Sibrandus* flew out with such raving and fierceness of countenance, and such unheard bitterness against

our

our Colledge, as I defire no other revenge on him, than the very speaking of the words, which while they were in his mouth were checked by the Prefident Politick, &c. In another letter, thus; The Palatine Divines are the onely Magistrates Doctors next to *Gomarus* in all the Synod, and think every thing they speak should be taken for Text. Let me adde one passage more, wherein *Gomarus* is mainly concerned; In the business of the Remonstrants of *Campes*, they of *Breme* perswaded to a middle course in dealing with them. But *Gomarus* (saith *Belcanqual*) fell foully upon *Martinus*, a man very learned and very honest, who hath been so uncivily dealt with, that the Forreigners take much offence thereat, and he and his Colleagues have been ready to leave the Synod. Because he dislikes, as others do the Contra-remonstrants broad speeches in many points, they use him with so much discourtesy; Though one be against the Remonstrants in all the 5 Articles in substance; yet if he differ from them [the *Dutch* Divines] but in manner of speaking, they hold him as not sound. So far *Belcanqual*; I thought not indeed to meddle with this business relating to them of *Breme*, but fell into it unawares, and cannot but learn from it, that if the Contra-remonstrants behaved themselves so, in such a place, against persons who in the main were of their perswafion, then certainly the Remonstrants to whom they were professed Adversaries, had cause to expect from them none of the softest usage. But there is one passage more that I shall

recite

recite out of *Belcanqual* concerning *Gomarus*. In Seſſion 85, *Gomarus* in his diſquiſition of the 3 and 4 Articles, delivered a ſpeech againſt the *Bremenſes*, which none I think but a mad man would have uttered, and he delivered himſelf with ſuch ſparkling of his eyes, and fierceneſs of pronunciation, as every man wondered that the Preſident did not cut him off; at laſt he cut off himſelf, I think for want of breath, and then the Preſident gave *celeberrimo Duo Gomaro* very many thanks for that his learned, grave and accurate ſpeech. The *Exteri* [the forreign Divines] wondered at it, *Martinus* onely ſaid, that he was ſorry he ſhould be ſo rewarded for his long journey. In another letter; All I will ſay my Lord, is this; There are two men in the Synod; *Sibrandus*, but eſpecially *Gomarus*, who are able to ſet it on fire, unleſs they be lookt to. Thus far he: I ſhall ſay nothing of the generality of the Provincial or *Dutch* Divines, how they were at the devotion of thoſe that were chief Actors in the Contra-remonſtratical Tragedy.

We are come now to the Execution of the Synodical Sentence againſt the Remonſtrants; They being thus diſcharged, other Paſtors were put and ſubſtituted in their places, how unwilling ſoever the Chuches were to receive them; In ſome places theſe new Paſtors were brought in by force of arms. Now leſt the ejected Remonſtrants ſhould teach privately, therefore the *States-General* propoſe to them a certain ingagement, to abſtain in the future both directly and indirectly from all even private

exerciſe

exercise of their Ministry. To which when some could not in conscience subscribe, they were condemned to perpetual banishment. Alas! who could expect such cruelty amongst Protestants, that had condemned Papists for the like unchristian practices? He that takes a view of our *Episcopius* and some others of the Remonstrants in their deportment, when this dismal Cloud appeared, will see cause to admire their faith and fortitude. For so dear was the truth unto them, and their zeal for it so great, that a promise of the same wages or stipend which they formerly enjoyed, could not induce them (though some of them had but a very mean Estate) to oblige and bind themselves unto silence, which was commanded them; Moreover these Generous spirits did with much boldness, after the pronouncing of the of sentence of Banishment, defend openly to the *States-General* their own and their associates Innocency, appealing to God, the avenger of them that are unjustly oppressed, who would at the last day take cognisance of their Cause, and judge, without respect of person, as well their Judges as them.

Hereupon these Stout Champions for truth were so hastily carryed away by the *States* Officers out of the limits of the *United Provinces*, that they after their detaining eight moneths at *Dort*, whether they were called, as they thought, to a free Synod, had not granted to them so much as one day, in which to bid their families farewell, and to set in order their domestick affairs

fairs, notwithstanding they petitioned for it. *Episcopius* therefore, and the rest, betook themselves to *Brabant*, and inhabited at *Antwerp*, during the peace between the King of *Spain* and the *States*. This place these Exiles made choice of for their abode, not to joyn with the enemies of their Country in a conspiracy against it, nor to endeavour any thing detremental to the Reformed religion, as some malevolent persons were bold enough to suggest slanderously against them; but because that place was near, and from which they might more commodiously, than from any place remote, take care of their beloved Churche, and Families. How faithfully those imployed their talent, received of God, I shall here pass over in Silence, being now to speak onely of *Episcopius*, whose disputations with *Peter Wadingus*, a *Jesuit* of *Antwerp*, and his Antidote against the Canons of the Synod of *Dort*, do abundanly testify his great care and diligence; And also the Confession of faith, which he, with the other Remonstrant Pastors there, did compose and publish, that they might stop the mouths of them who calumniously gave forth, that the Remonstrants cherisht in their breast, monstrous and strange opinions, which they durst not expose to publick view.

When the war was renewed between the *King* of *Spain* and the *States*, our *Episcopius*, seeing he could no longer with safety remain in *Brabant*, departed

departed thence into *France*, and inhabited sometime at *Rhoan*, sometime at *Paris*. If thou inquire how in these parts his time was spent, those Writings of his there compiled, will give thee a worthy Account, in case thou art able to peruse his *Paraphrase* and *Observations* on the 8, 9, 10, and 11 *Chapters* of St. *Pauls Epistle* to the *Romans*; also his *Bodecherus ineptiens*; his *Examen Thesium Jacobi Capelli*; his answer to to the *Defence of Jo. Cameron*; his *Treatise of Christian Magistracy*, and that of *free-will*, with other works of his, laboured there. He that with these considers his sollicitous Care for the Churches of his own Countrey, which in this time of persecution being destitute of their ordinary Pastors, he by diverse Writings and Epistles instructed, comforted and incouraged to persevere in the Faith; also the many conferences he had with learned men concerning Religion, by which he endeavoured to bring them to a more accurate search and inquiry after the truth; he, I say, that considers these things, will be so far from thinking that he had many wast hours that he will greatly wonder, where time was found for so many and great Atchievments. Here *Stephen Curcellæus* got with him his first Acquaintance and professes that he heard him discourse of some hard points of religion, and learned so many things of him, that he always afterwards esteemed it a singular happpiness to him, that he had acquaintance with so worthy a man Here also *Episcopius* contracted such a friendship with that most cordial man and eminent Mathematician, Mr. *Edmund Mercer*, which afterwards no distance of place, or length of time, could dissolve or weaken. This was he that published this Book, by which *Camerons* opinion of Grace and free-will is examined, and intituled it, *Epistola viri docti*; and he that was so familiar a friend with *Hugo Grotius*, that *Grotius*, when he last left *France*, committed to him the most precious Treasures he had, his Elaborate Manuscripts, that by him they might be communicated to others.

At length *Episcopius*, being desirous to have a perfect Survay of *France*, who as yet knew little more than the Northern part of it, went from *Paris* to *Lyons*; After that he visited *Marseille*, *Nismes*, *Mompelier*, *Tholouse*: Afterwards *Burdeaux*, *Rochella*, *Poictiers*, *Angiers*, *Tours*, *Orleance*, and other places. And when he had finished his perambulation, he returned to *Paris* and *Rhoan*; where when he had remained a while; and had heard that the fervour of the persecution, raised in his own Countrey against the Remonstrants, was somewhat alayed, he purposed to return thither. Leaving therefore *France* in the year of our Lord 1626, and in the eighth year of his banishment, he came to *Rotterdam*, that he might with other brethren lay out his abilities for the gathering of that very numerous Church, which is there out of the dispersed Remonstrants: And that afterwards he might take care for other Churches in the *United Provinces*

Provinces. In the mean while by his Writings both in Latin and Dutch he strenuously defended the truth. He published in Latin An Apology of the Remonstrants confession; An Answer to the Essay of the *Leyden Professors*, with other Books. In *Dutch* he wrote a Treatise of true Antiquity against the Papists; Three Treatises against *James Triglandius*, then Preacher at *Amsterdam*; since Professor of Divinity at *Leyden*; with other books.

In the second year after his return, he entred into a Matrimonial state, (there being then hope of a more peaceable time) marrying at *Rotterdam* that most choice and vertuous Gentlewoman Mrs. *Mary Peffer*, the widow of Mr. *Henry Niellius* a Preacher of that City, and the younger brother of Mr. *Charles Niellius* above-mentioned. They lived together, but without issue, most piously, peaceably and comfortably to the end of the years 1641, at which time she finished her course.

But before this in the year 1634 He went to *Amsterdam*, to be President in the Remonstrants Scholastick Nursery or Colledge, which was erected there to be as an University, for the instructing of Youth in Divinity, that were intended for Ministers of the Church.

How faithfully and diligently he exercised himself here, we have an illustrious testimony from his copious, learned and most usefull Theological Institutions; and the Answer of 64 Questions

pro-

proposed to him by his Disciples; also from his learned and eloquent Sermons to the people; also his true Remonstrant Divine; and his Answer to the 10 Dilemma's of a certain Popish Doctor, and other works of his.

Whilest he was thus labouring, some occasions forced him to *Rotterdam*, where *Anno* 1639 he fell dangerously sick, and for some moneths kept his bed, and so far was he gone, that there was little hope of his recovery. But at length God restored him to health, and so strengthened him, that he returned to his charge at *Amsterdam*, and as diligently laboured among them as before.

After his return it seemed good to the Remonstrants to publish a plain Catechism for the instructing of the more ignorant sort. Then *Abraham Heydan*, at that time a Preacher at *Leyden*, afterwards Professor of Divinity there, published an Examination of this Catechism, the defence of which our *Episcopius* undertook, and finished in a considerable large Volume, which came not forth till after his death. For in the beginning of the year 1643, when he was well nigh 60 years old, he fell mortally sick. His disease is called *Ischuria*, a dangerous suppression of the *Urine*, which was so pertinacious and obstinate, that for eleven days he could not make one drop of water, although some skilfull Physicians used the utmost of their art to master, or at least somewhat to mitigate this his mercyless and stubborn enemy. This Excrement (of which he afterward avoided but little) mixing it self with the blood of the whole body, so corrupted the *Crassis* and temperature thereof, that he could not possibly long subsist.

He lay sick two moneths and above, and for some weeks before his death was deprived of sight. Which loss, whilest there was any hope of his recovery, had been exceeding grievous unto him, had not his deep and almost continual sleeping lessened the same; For sometimes he complained of it to his friends that did frequently visit him, saying, that he should not be able any more to serve the Church of Christ.

At length on the 4th of *April* about the 8th hour in the morning, (at which time the moon was in the Eclipse) he peaceably fell asleep in the Lord. And the 4th day after was carryed forth (a great multitude of all sorts of persons following the herse) unto the West-Church, and was there interred by his wife. His death many much lamented, and many Epicedium's, or funeral Verses of his praise and commendation, were published both in *Dutch* and *Latin*.

Caspar Barlæus, the most renowned Poet of that time, and who lived not full two years after him, published a most excellent *Latin Epicedium*

dium in his commendation, which is prefixed to the first Volume of *Episcopius* his works.

Thus we have taken a short view of *Episcopius* from his birth to his death. His life was unblameable, and illustrious for zeal to the glory of God, and mans salvation; His Love to the Churches peace and concord added much to his commendation. He was indeed much conversant in Controversies, not of choyce, but through necessity; He was often wont to complain of his constraint to this kind of exercise. His patient bearing of injuries, and readiness to forgive, after the example of his Master Christ, contributed not a little to his praise. In alms-deeds he was to his power ready and cheerfull; And such was his modesty and humble temper, that his rare endowments and great Atchievments he esteemed as nothing. On his sick-bed his Speeches were gracious, full of piety towards God, charity towards men and confidence in Christ. His name now and memory is blessed with them especially, that without prejudice peruse his works, that in two considerable Volumes are now publick in the Latin tongue, which I could wish that all men well understood, were it but to read *Episcopius*. I doubt not but there are many, who have much improved themselves by his writings. Our famous *Hales* is not doubtless without companions of whom this is reported by Mr.

Anthony

Anthony Farindon, his familiar friend; that he himself often told him, that at the well pressing of *Jo.* 3, 16. by *Episcopius*, he bade *Jo. Calvine* Good-night. It would be in vain for me here to inlarge, who am speaking to those, that through unacquaintance with Latin, are uncapable to see the great knowledge and eloquence of our *Episcopius*: as for those who converse honestly with his Writings, they need not me. But I would not that any should think of me, that I take all his sayings for gospel; No, I believe that his Writings as well as other mens must be read with judgment: for I nothing doubt, but that Errata's may be found in his works, not only such that are justly imputable to the Transcriber and Printer, but such also that are the Authors, who was subject to erre, though much more free from errors than many.

FINIS.

Books Printed for *Francis Smith* at the *Elophant* and *Castle* without *Temple-bar*.

Baptism before or after Faith and Repentance largely discussed; not onely in publick Disputations, Managed by many Ministers before Thousands of people, but also Mr. *Baxter*, Dr. *Holmes*, Dr. *Featly*, Mr. *Marshall*, Mr. *Blake*, Mr. *Cook*, Mr. *Cotton*; Their arguments for and against truly controverted being a subject very useful in these inquiring times, for general satisfaction in this point so much controverted, in *folio* 10 s. 6. d.

Hooles Latin and English Grammer, fitted not onely for the use of all Schools, but very usefull for any person desirous to Learn the Latin tongue, being a more plain and speedy help then any yet extant Sixth Edition; 8º. *price bound 2 s.*

A Caution to Christians against Mistakes in their Faith, opening the nature and difference of effectual faith that will not, and of the Dead faith that will at last deceive men in their hopes of Justification by it; shewing also that holiness in men as well as the happiness of men is Gods aim in Contriving the tearms of their Salvation in 4o, 2 s. 6 d. bound.

One thing needfull, or a serious meditation on the 4 last things, Death, Judgment, Heaven and Hell

Hell unto which is now added *Eball* and *Gerizzim;* or the Blessing and the Curse. third Edition 12º. 6. d. bound.

The Young Scholars pocket.Book containing the first Rudiments in Arithmetick, with the Rule of 3. also the way to find the Content of Board, Glass, Land, Timber, Stone, Globes. third Edition, 12º. 8. d. bound.

Youths Tragedy, a Poem drawn up by way of Dialogue, between Youth, the Devil, Wisdom, the Nuncius, Time, Death, the Soul, for Caution and Direction of the younger sort. third Edition 4º. 4. d. bound.

Symptomes of growth and decay to Godliness, in 80 Signs of a living and dying Christian, with the causes of decay and remedies for recoveries in Large 8º. third Edition at 1. s. 6. d. bound.

A new and usefull Concordance to the Holy Bible, whereunto is added beyond any extant the chief acceptations and various significations of words contained in the Old and new Testament, with marks to distinguish the Commands, promises and Threatnings; also a collection of those Scripture prophesies which relate to the Call of the Jews and the Glory that shall be in the Latter Days in 8º. at 2. s. 6. d. bound. in 12º. at 2. s. bound. where it is also to be had printed on a fine page and bound with the Bible in 8º. or 12º.

FINIS.

THE JUDGMENT

OF

Mr. *Francis Bamfield*,
late Minister of *Sherborne* in *Dorsetshire*

FOR THE

Observation of the *Jewish*,

OR

Seventh Day SABBOTH:

With his Reasons and Scriptures for the same.
Sent in a Letter to

Mr. *Ben* of *Dorchester*.

TOGETHER

With Mr. *Benn*'s sober Answer to the same; and a Vindication of the *Christian Sabboth* against the *Jewish*.

Published for the Satisfaction of divers Friends in the West of *England*.

Revelations 1. 10.
I was in the Spirit on the Lords Day.

LONDON,
Printed by *W. Godbid*, for *Joseph Nevill* at the *Gray-Hound* in St Paul's-Church-Yard, 1672.

The Preface.

Christian Reader,

IN *times when People are generally debauched in their Intellectuals as well as in their Morals, and take as great a liberty of opining as they do of practising, it is no wonder if in this Age, when as all Sects seem to have a general resurrection, that the* Jewish *Sect have also their Abettors; but if People would but seriously consider, that the change of the Day hath the same Foundation that the Scriptures themselves have (and that is Catholick Tradition) the Controversie would quickly be at an end: It would then be an easie thing to believe, that when the whole* Jewish *Frame of Worship was laid aside, it was fit that the very time it self should also put on Mourning, and therefore well may it pass for a Fast*

The Preface.

as our Church hath rightly instituted it: but to continue it as a Feast to the Lord, is to put an Affront upon the Gospel and the whole Oeconomy of it. And therefore if this Tract may contribute any thing, either to the confirming those that stand, or the establishing those that are ready to fall, or recovering of those that are already gone astray, the Author hath his end, and desires the to give God all the Glory.

Honoured Sir,

I Understand by some others, who report it to me, as from you, That you desire some Scriptures may be put to those particulars which I formerly sent you, wherein I gave you an account of my Judgement, which accordingly here I have done. If any do think fit to examine this Paper, and to return me an Answer in Writing, I expect that he should consider it as it doth stand in order, and declare expresly his Assent and Consent to the several Particulars, if he be convinced that they are the mind of GOD in his Word; or if he Dissent, that he give the Reasons thereof in a Scripture-way.

My Judgement, according to the Scriptures, is as followeth, That

1. *First*, Jehovah Christ, by the appointment of the Father, and by the anointing of the Spirit, is established for ever to be the only Lord over the Conscience, and Law-giver to the Soul, *Isa.* 33. 22. To shew that this is meant of the Lord Christ, compare *Isa.* 32. 1, 15. and 33. 17, 18. and 42. 1, 4, 16, 21. the 18. verse of the 33. chap. of *Isa.* is applyed by the Apostle in 1 *Cor.* 1. 20. to the times of the Gospel, so also is *Isa.* 42. 1, 2, 3, 4. applyed by Christ to himself, *Matth.* 12. 17, 21. *Gal.* 6. 2. *Jam.* 2. 8, 10, 11, 12. and 4. 12. *Rom.* 14. 9, 11. *Heb.* 12. 2, 6. *Deut.* 18. 18. *Joh.* 16. 13, 14, 15. *Acts* 3. 22, 23. *Isa.* 8. 10, 16, 20. 1 *Cor.* 12. 3. *Mat.* 12. 18. *Mark* 2. 28. *Luke* 6. 5. *Matth.* 17. 5. *Acts* 7. 37, 38. *Psal.* 68. 8, 11, 17, 18. *Psal.* 2. *Matth.* 28. 18, 19, 20.

2dly.

2dly. Secondly, The holy Scriptures of truth are perfect, full, and sufficient in all cases whatsoever, of Doctrine, of Worship, of Discipline, of Government, and of Conversation, 2 *Tim.* 3. 15, 16, 17. *Rev.* 22. 18, 19. compared with *Deut.* 4. 12. *Prov.* 30. 6. *Mark* 7. 7, 13. *Deut.* 12. 32. *Levit.* 18. 34. *Deut.* 17. 15, 20. *Josh.* 11. 8. *Joh.* 20. 30, 31. *Gal.* 3. 15. *Matth.* 22. 9.

3dly. Thirdly, The Ten words are a perfect and compleat, standing, unchangeable Rule of Life, in all matters of Duty to be peformed, and of Sin to be avoided, *Psal.* 19. 7, 8, 9. *Isa.* 8. 20. *Rom.* 3. 20. and 4. 15. 1 *Joh.* 3. 4. *Deut.* 12. 32. 1 *Pet.* 1. 23, 25. *Deut.* 4. 1, 2, 13. *Luke* 16. 29, 30. *Deut.* 5. 22. *Exod.* 1. 27, 28. and 31. 18. *Psal.* 119. throughout, and particularly *vers.* 126, 151. *Joh.* 20. 35. *Jam.* 1. 25. *Prov.* 8. 8, 9. *Matth.* 15. 17, 19. *Rom.* 3. 31. 1 *Joh.* 2. 7.

4thly. Fourthly, The Seventh day, which is the last day in every Week

[ ]

in the weekly returns of it, is alone that particular, peculiar day in every week, which is the weekly Sabbath day, to be kept holy to Jehova, in obedience to his Command as such, *Exod.* 20. 8, 9. *Deut.* 5. 12, 15.

1. *First*, Because those weighty Reasons which Jehova the Law giver himself hath given to enforce Obedience to his Command, in observing a weekly Sabbath day holy to himself, do properly and only belong, and are applicable to the Seventh day, which is the last day in every Week, in order of time, in the weekly returns of it, as a weekly Sabbath day; and to no other day in the week, *Exod.* 20. 11.

1. *First*, God rested only upon the Seventh day, which is the last day in the week, and upon no other day in the week as a weekly Sabbath day; *Exod.* 20. 1. and 31. 15, 17. compare *Gen.* 1. throughout, particularly *vers.* 5, 8, 13, 31. with *chapt.* 2. 1, 2, 3. *Heb.* 4. 3, 4. *Exod.* 16. 23, 30. *Lev.* 23. 3. 2*dly*.

[5]

2*dly.* Secondly, God bleſſed only the Seventh day, which is the laſt day of the week, and no other day of the week, as a weekly Sabbath day; *Exod.* 20. 10, 11. compared with *Gen.* 2. 2, 3.

3*dly.* Thirdly, God ſanctified only the ſeventh day, which is the laſt day of the week, and no other day of the week as a weekly Sabbath day; *Exod.* 20. 10, 11. compared with *Gen.* 2. 2, 3.

2*dly.* Secondly, Becauſe all the Scriptures throughout where the holy Spirit ſpeaketh of a weekly Sabbath day.

1. Firſt, The name and thing of a weekly Sabbath day is given only to the Seventh, which is the laſt day in the weekly returns of it, and to no other day in the week as a weekly Sabbath day; *Deut.* 5. 14. *Exod.* 20. 10. and 16. 25, 26. and 31. 15. and 35. 1. *Lev.* 23. 3. *Acts* 16. 13. and 17. 2. and 18. 4. *Luke* 4. 16. *Matth.* 24. 20.

2*dly.* Secondly, There is no Command

mand given for the obfervation of any other day in the week as a weekly Sabbath day to Jehovah but only the feventh, which is the laft day of the week in the weekly returns of it; *Exod.* 20. 8,11. *Deut.* 5. 12, 15. *Exod.* 16. 28. and 34. 31. and 35. 12. and 23. 12. and 31. 13,14,15. *Levit.* 19. 3,30. and 23. 3. and 26. 2. *Neh.* 9. 14. *Jer.* 17. 21, 22. *Matth.* 28. 18,19,20. *Ezek.* 20. 19, 20. and 44. 24. *Luke* 23. 5, 6. *Levit.* 10. 1. *Jer.* 7. 23, 31.

3*dly*. Thirdly, There is no Promife made to the obfervation of any other day of the week, as a weekly Sabbath day, but only of the feventh, which is the laft day of the week in the weekly returns of it; *Ifa.* 56.1,8. and 58. 13, 18. *Jer.* 17. 24, 25, 26. *Levit.* 26. 2,13. *Exod* 16.29. *Mark* 2.27. *Ezek.* 20. 20.

4*thly*. Fourthly, There is no Threatning either denounced againft, or execrated upon any that fhall not observe

observe any other day, as a weekly Sabbath day, but only the Seventh day which is the last day of the week in the weekly returns of it; *Exod.* 20. 9, 10. and 31. 13, 14, 15. and 35. 3. *Jer.* 17. 27. *Exod.* 20. 21. *Nehem.* 13. 15, 21.

3*dly.* Thirdly, Because God hath put this into Nature, *Exod.* 20. 10. *thy Stranger*; *Deut.* 5. 14. the three first Chapters to the *Romans*, particularly, *chap.* 2. 14, 15, 26, 27. and 3. 9, 20. 1 *Cor.* 11. 14. Nature hath its teachings; the Humane nature in the first *Adam* was made and framed to the perfection of the Ten Words, some notions whereof are still retained, even in the Corrupt state of fallen Man; compare *Gen.* 1. 26, 27. *Eccles.* 7. 29. *Ephes.* 4. 20. *Col.* 3. 10.

The Law of the seventh day Sabbath was given before the Law was proclaimed at *Sinai*, *Exod.* 16. 23. even from the Creation, *Gen.* 2. 2, 3. given to to *Adam* in respect of his Humane nature, and in him to all the World of humane creatures; compare *Gen.* 1. 14. and *Psal.* 104. 19. with *Levit.* 25. 21. and *Num.* 28. 2, 9, 10. it is the same word in the Original *Mognadim*, contracted, *Mognade.*

Set times of Divine appointment for solemn Assembling, and for Gods instituted Service, are directed to, and pointed at by those great Lights which the Creator hath set up in the Heavens; *Psal.* 19. throughout, compared with *Rom.* 10. 4, 5, 6, 7, 8, 18, 19, 20. *Deut.* 30. 10, 15. *Joh.* 1. 9. Every man hath a Law and Light of Nature which he carrieth about him, and is born and bred together with him; Those seeds of Light and Truth, *Rom.* 1. 20. though they will not Justifie him in the sight of God, and bring a Soul through, and safe home to Glory, yet there, even since *Adam*'s fall, are those reliques and

dark

dark letters of His holy Law of the Ten words to preserve the memory of our first created Dignity, and for some other ends, though these Seeds are utterly corrupted now, *Tit.* 1. 15. Natural Reason will tell men, that seeing all men in all Nations do measure their times by Weeks, and their weeks by Seven days, they should (besides what they offer up of their time, as due to God every day) give one whole day of every Week to their Maker, who hath allowed them so liberal a portion of time, therein to provide for themselves ; (there being no other proportion of time that can so well provide for the necessities of Families, as Six dayes of every Week, and that is so well fitted to all functions, callings, and employments.) And the light of Nature, when cleared up, will tell men, That all labour and motion being in order to rest, and rest being the perfection

and

and end of labour, into which labour, work, and motion doth pass, that therefore the Seventh, which is the last day in every Week, is the fittest and properest day for a religious Rest, unto the Creator, for his Worship and Service; *Gen.* 2. 1, 2, 3. *Exod.* 20. 9, 10, 11. *Deut.* 5. 13, 14. *Heb.* 4. 1, 11. *Exod.* 31. 7. *Rom.* 14. 13, *Exod.* 23. 12. and 34. 2. Nature doth suggest that man and beast, should have a Resting-day every Week, *Deut.* 5. 14.

The Lord Christs obedience unto this *fourth Word*, in observing in his life time the Seventh day as a Weekly Sabbath-day, which is the last day of the Week in the weekly returns of it, and no other day of the Week as such, is a part of that perfect Righteousness which every sound Believer doth apply to himself, in order to his being Justified in the sight of God; and every such person is to conform unto

Christ

Christ in all the acts of Obedience to the Ten Words; *Luke* 4.16. *Rom.* 8. 2, 3, 4. and 5. 12. *Gal.* 4. 4, 5. 2 *Cor.* 5. 21. *Jer.* 23. 6. *Rev.* 19. 8. *Isa.* 45. 23, 24, 25. *Rom.* 6. throughout, 1 *Pet.* 2. 21. *Ephes.* 5. 1, 2. 1 *Joh.* 2. 3, 4. 1 *Joh.* 1. 6. 1 *Joh.* 2. 1, 6. and 4. 17. *Iohn* 15. 10, 12, 14. *Matth.* 11. 28, 29, 30. *Iohn* 13. 34. *Heb.* 12. 2.

Francis Bampfield.

Mr. BEN'S ANSVVER TO Mr. BAMPFIELD'S PAPER.

The will of Gods good pleasure is the sole Rule and reason of all his actings towards the Creature.

The holy Will of God revealed in his holy Word is the sole Rule and Measure of all the Creatures actings towards God.

He-

Honoured Sir, and very much Reverenced in the Lord,

GReat is the Obligation you have laid upon me, in condescending so far as to communicate unto me those Scripture grounds and reasons, which have had such an irresistable influence upon your Conscience, as to undergo such a change in your Judgment and Practice, relating to the observation of the Weekly Sabbath, from what you have formerly believed and practised, and that I am fully perswaded in Godly sincerity: This, Sir, is as I understand the discourse of many, the wonder of not a few, and the grief of some.

I do acknowledge, that the report which you say was brought unto you, was true; I did indeed desire that you would be pleased at your leisure, if you thought good, to adde some Scripture-proofs to those Propositions which I had formerly received from you: which I think I
B should

should not have taken the boldness to have done; but that you had given me encouragement, as I suppose you remember when, and where, and how; which now that you have done, I shall endeavour to observe your order in giving you my thoughts of them, and that, as they stand in your Paper; and according to your desire, expresly declare my assent, and consent to the several particulars, so far as I am convinced that they are according to the mind of God; and wherein I dissent to give you my reasons thereof, and yet as you expect in a Scripture way, so far as I am able and understand the meaning of that expression, and submit all to your serious examination.

1. Concerning your three first Propositions, I do both heartily assent, and unfeignedly consent unto you, so far as I apprehend aright your mind in them, as divine truths of infallible veracity, deeply engraven in the Word of Truth. Oh that they were as deeply engraven in the hearts of all the Lords professing people! Only I crave leave to tell you,

1. That whereas for the proof of the first, That Jehovah Christ is by the appointment

pointment of the Father, &c. whereas, I say, for the proof of this you quote, if I mistake not, near about 26 Scriptures, I cannot either assent or consent, that every one of them speaks clearly to the confirmation of the Proposition, possibly they are mis written by the Transcriber; however the Truth is sufficiently confirmed by some of them, and I think all of them may afford matter of comfortable meditation for the right improvement of Christs Kingly Office, which perhaps is all that you intend by them. Blessed be the Lord, the Government is upon his shoulder, *Isa.* 9. 8. that he is the King of Nations, *Jer.* 10. 17. that he is the King of Saints, *Rev.* 15. 3 head over all things to the Church, *Eph.* 1. 22. hath power over all flesh, to give eternal life to all those the Father hath given him, *Joh.* 17. 2. That Scripture (which is well observed by you) in *Isa.* 33. 32. is much to be taken notice of; for understand the words in a Spiritual sence, and they are exclusive of all other; *Christ alone, Christ and no other, is our only King, and our only Law-giver.* It is true, the Commands of the Magistrate bind the Conscience, and we must be subject for Conscience sake, *Rom.* 13. 5. yet not immediately, but by the intervention of Gods Command, *Rom.* 13. 1, 2. nor yet universally, but with limitation; we must obey the Lord Christ, upon the bare sight of his will: but the Laws of men, are farther to be considered of, that so our obedience unto them may be without scruple, and our subjection not from self-interest, but in deed and in truth, from principles of Conscience.

2dly. Whereas for the proof of the second Proposition, that the holy Scripture of truth is a perfect and sufficient rule, for Doctrine, Worship, and Discipline, you produce eleven or twelve Scriptures: thus far I consent that the proposition is true, and sufficiently proved, though some of the Scriptures are upon some account or other, mistaken or misquoted; as *Gal.* 3. 15. which perhaps you intend for *Gal.* 6. 16. The one speaks not to the point, as the other doth; from the latter *Chemnitius*, as I remember, conceives that the Scriptures may be said to be Canonical; they are indeed a perfect Canon, nothing to be added thereunto, not by any Revelation

from

from the spirit, much less from any human Traditions, 2 *Thes.* 3. 2. *Gal.* 1. 8, 9. If an Angel from Heaven preach any other Doctrine, let him, saith the Apostle, again, and again he saith it, let him be accursed. Yet I think this limitation is fit to be inserted, that there are some Circumstances concerning Worship, and Administration of Church affairs (such I mean, as are common to humane Actions and Societies) which are to be ordered by Christian prudence, but still according to the general rules of the word, which ought alwayes to be observed, that so as, 1 *Cor.* 14. 40. *All things may be done decently and in order*: that [*all things*] that is, all the Ordinances of God, for of them he speaks, as appears in the foregoing verses: *Prayer and singing of Psalms* &c. This text gives no other power to any Church, or Church-Governors, but that all such things as God appoints, be done decently without uncomliness, and orderly without confusion.

3*dly*. That whereas for the proof of the third Proposition, That the ten words are a perfect, compleat, and standing rule, &c. you produce at least twenty Scriptures: I

both

both Assent, and Consent, acknowledging the Proposition sufficiently proved; though I must say, as I said before, that every particular text which is quoted, comes not up fully to prove the point, but a divine truth, it is beyond all contradiction, that as, *Psal.* 119. 96. the Commands are exceeding broad, containing an infinite, and incomprehensible treasure of heavenly wisdom perteining to holiness, nothing is wanting that is necessary for direction to all men, in all conditions, being it is an eternal rule of righteousness; and as *Matth.* 24. 31. *Heaven and Earth shall pass away, but my word,* saith the Lord Jesus Christ, *shall not pass away.* Thus God hath magnified his Law, and made it honourable, *Isa.* 42. 21. Thus you see, how in truth of these three propositions I consent with you.

4*thly*. But now for the fourth Proposition, that the seventh day, which is the last day in every week, in the weekly revolution, is alone that peculiar day in every week, which is the weekly Sabbath day, to be kept holy to *Jehovah* in obedience to his Commands. For the proof whereof you bring *Exod.* 20. 8, 9, 10, 11. *Deut.* 5. 12, 13.

13. to this I must crave leave to say; that as yet I can neither Assent, nor Consent, being no wayes convinced by any thing I find in your paper, that is according to the mind of God, revealed in his word, or proved in the least, either by these Scriptures, or the reasons produced for the proof thereof.

That which takes hold of my Conscience, in this matter I shall lay before you, when I have,

1. First told you, what is the General, I observe in your paper.

2. Secondly given you some few propositions, which I think meet to be inserted here, to avoid repetitions hereafter.

1. I observe, that all your Arguments are grounded upon a strong apprehension you are under, that the seventh day, the last day in every week, is the substance of the fourth Commandment: And that it is moral natural, written in the Humane nature in *Adam*, which was framed to the perfection of the ten words, as you express it in your third general reason. But in this, I can neither Assent, nor Consent: The reason of my Dissent, you shall have in its proper place; I mean, why I conceive,

ceive, that though the Humane nature in *Adam* was made after the Image of God in righteoufnefs, and true holynefs; yet the law for the laft day of feven in every week to be the only day for the weekly Sabbath, was not written there.

2dly. I obferve, that your apprehenfions are ftrong, that the laft day of feven in every week, and the Sabbath day, that is, the day of holy reft of Gods appointment for his folemn worfhip in every week, are and muft be termes Convertible, and that the laft of feven in every week, as it was at firft, fo it is now, and muft fo continue, to the end of the world, is the only day for that purpofe. This I gather from thofe Reafons given to inforce obedience to the Commands which you fay properly belong to this day, and are, as you think, applicable to no other day: herein I can neither affent nor confent, and why I cannot, I fhall give you my grounds, when I have firft confidered the propofitions you lay down before them.

3dly. I obferve, and that not without fome wonder, that though the whole ftrefs of all your Arguments, is in a manner, laid upon the 9, 10, 11, verfes of *Exod.* 20.

20. Yet I find nothing at all Argumentatively to prove, that the scope, sence, and meaning of these words, is to establish the last of seven, in the revolution of every week, to be the only day of holy rest, which is to be observed to *Jehovah*, to the end of the world; which is the proposition you engage your self to make good; which till you have done by some other Arguments than this paper affords, or by these Arguments more clearly; I do believe that what you now assert, will not be so generally received for truth, according to the minde of God, as you think it ought, and as it ought, if it be indeed the mind of God in his word.

2*dly*. Having observed these things, I now crave leave to lay down some few propositions, which being considered of, may be, according to what I apprehend, of some use, (they are at least to me) towards the clearing up of the matter under debate, and meet to be inserted here, to avoid as you said, as much as may be, repetitions hereafter. They are as followeth.

1. First, That all dayes materially considered in themselves, are equal, and of the

the same nature in that respect, none more necessary to be observed than another; none more subservient to any spiritual advantage than another; every day had the same efficient cause, all being created by God, and all very good, *Gen.* 1. all ruled and governed by him, and filled up with what providential dispensation seemed good in his sight, *Psal.* 47. 16. Thus all dayes considered as I say materially in themselves, now and ever will be alike: As they were under the Law, so under the Gospel, none of them more eminent nor observable by any natural goodness than another. If this be so, and I think it cannot be denyed but that it is so, this will be one strong argument, as I apprehend, to prove that the last day of seven in every week, to be the only, and perpetual day for the day of weekly holy rest unto *Jehovah*, was not written in the humane nature in *Adam* in the state of Innnocency, as I hope to make evident when I come to speak to the third general reason.

2dly. Secondly, That though the letter of the Text ought alway to be carefully heeded, yet alway to stick to it, and never compare Scripture with Scripture, for the

better

better understanding of the sence thereof, may prove a dangerous snare. This hath been the Butt of Contention between the *Lutherans* and the *Calvinists*, and this hath been the death of many faithfull Martyrs, by the Popish Generation, when and where they had power in their hands, the one holding too pertinaciously to the letter of the Text, *Mat.* 26.26. *This is my body*, for the maintaining of Transubstantiation; a sad instance we have of this in that Conference at *Hussia*, at *Marpurgus*, I remember (for the Book I have not by me) between *Luther*, *Melanchton*, *Zuinglius*, *Oecolampadius*, *Bucer*, and other *German* Divines, as it is related in the Annals of *Soultetus*, where we read, that even *Luther* himself rejected very strong reasons, against which he had nothing to say but *Hoc est corpus meum*; this if the Translator of his *Mensalia* hath not wronged him, he receded from that opinion before his death: So the Popish Commentators sticking to the letter of the Text, *Jam.* 2. 14. where it is said, that a man is justified by Works, and not by Faith only, so far as they are believed, overturn the foundation of Faith: The like

like in part may be said of sticking to the letter of the fourth Commandment, without minding the scope, sence, and meaning of it: I think thereby a man shall cast a mist before his eyes, which will exceedingly hinder him from the right understanding of the mind of God therein: If I should do so, I should find it to be so. This being so, makes way for a third Proposition, which thus I lay down.

3*dly*. Thirdly, Though all things necessary to be known, believed, and observed, in order to Salvation, are clearly revealed (though not altogether, but) in one place or other of the Scripture, so that persons of ordinary capacities in the right use of means, assisted by the holy spirit of God, may attain a sufficient understanding of them, so as not to perish for want of knowledge; yet all truths are not alike plain in themselves, nor alike clear to all: some things are hard to be understood, 2 *Pet.* 3. 16. which though *Peter* (speaking no doubt upon his own knowledge) saith some misconstrued to their own ruine; yet, which is worthy our observation, neither doth he, nor *Paul* himself (who was yet alive, as seemed by that expression in

the

the former part of the verſe (*our beloved brother Paul*) and in all probability knew as much in this matter as *Peter* did) neither of them I ſay, did clear or amend theſe difficulties, but let them alone as they were. Thus it ſeemed good to the holy ſpirit of God, by whoſe inſpiration the Scripture was written, to have it ſo: ſome truths are as if it were hid under the rock, that ſo there might be digging and ſearching after the knowledg of them, *as for hid Treaſures*, *Prov.* 2. 4. and if I ſay that the ſecond and fourth Commandments may be reckoned amongſt ſuch truths, I think I ſhould have many that would ſay ſo too; I have reaſon to ſay, they have been both ſo to me, but bleſſed be the Lord for that light, how little ſoever, I have received in the one or in the other. Doubtleſs it concerns us therefore to be much in prayer, that God would open our eyes, that we might underſtand the wonderful things of his law, *Pſal.* 119.10. The vaile that was upon the hearts of the Jews in reading the Old Teſtament, 2 *Cor.* 3. 14, 15. is not fully removed from the hearts of the moſt knowing Chriſtians to this day: he that knows moſt, hath cauſe to acknowledge he knows but in part,

part, 2 *Cor.* 13. therefore I may propose, but I dare not impose any of my apprehensions upon others.

4*thly.* Fourthly, I desire this may be observed, which I suppose will not be denied, that a proof drawn by comparing Scripture with Scripture, or by necessary consequence from Scripture rightly understood, is a sufficient Scripture proof, even of that which in express words is not found in Scripture: That which we have, *Jam.* 4. 5. is no where that I can see found in Scripture, in so many express words and syllables, but the truth contained therein is clear; therefore the Apostle saith that the Scripture saith, that the Spirit that is in us lusteth to envy: Many such instances might be given, evidently proving, that Inferences rightly deduced, are to be valued as express Scripture. In *Mat.* 22. 32. the Lord Christ himself proves the Resurrection of the Just, not by express Scripture, but by consequence. Thus for the Baptizing of Infants, and many other things which come frequently under observation, we have not express Scripture for, or in full, and entire sentences together, but here a little, and there a little,

which

which compared together, and wisely and faithfully improved by rational Inferences, sufficiently prove that Truth they are brought for: And if the Divine institution of the first day of the week, can be thus cleared up, for the day of the weekly Sabbath, as I doubt not but it may, it is sufficient to me it is.

He that conceives himself under no obligation to any thing, but what he hath express Scripture for, in so many words and syllables, will either enlarge his liberty beyond its due bounds, or streighten his rule beyond what is written, and perhaps both: its a dangerous thing to refuse him that speaks from Heaven, which way soever he speaks, *Heb.* 12. 25.

5*thly.* Fifthly, Let this be also considered, that the holy will of God, which is the rule of all righteousness, concerning what is required of man to do, hath been revealed, though the time when, and manner how it hath been revealed, be not recorded in Scripture. This to me is certain, for the will of God concerning Sacrificing, was without doubt revealed unto *Abel*, before the Law for Sacrifices was given; for what he did therein, he did in

Faith,

Faith, and eminently found acceptance with God in what he did therein, *Heb.* 11. 4. neither the Light of Nature, which is the knowledge of Principles, neither the Law of Nature, which is the conclusions drawn from these Principles, could ever have made known this way of worship to be a Duty, if God had not some way revealed his will to him therein. This I hope will be made evident when I come to speak of the third general Reason.

If he had imposed this upon himself, and that it had been the product of his own imagination, it had been will-worship: therefore certainly he had some word for it, but when he received it, and where, and how that way of worship was instituted for him to come to the knowledge of, I never heard of any that could find it in the Scripture. Great use may be made of this, if need were, for the clearing up of this present Controversie, concerning an express word for the institution and observing of the first day of the week to be the Lords-day, the day for his weekly Sabbath; we might say, that it might be instituted, though it be not recorded when,

when, and where, as it was in the case of *Abels* Sacrificing; but I hope we shall not be driven to this, however I cannot but suppose it is good use for some especially to consider of.

6thly. Sixthly, I desire that this also may be considered, that what was delivered by the Apostles, as they were guided by the holy Spirit of Truth, ought to be received and believed as delivered and spoken by Christ himself.

Christ himself was never in person at *Ephesus*, and yet 'tis said, *Eph.* 2. 17. that he came thither and preached peace unto them: we must understand it, that he did so in the Ministry of the Apostles, which was all one as if he had been there himself. None that I know of durst ever undertake to prove, that ever they prescribed any thing for all the Churches to observe, but what they received in Commission from the Lord Jesus. This was their charge, *Mat.* 28. 20. *Teach what I command you*; and this was their practice, 1 *Cor.* 11. 10, 23. *What I received from the Lord, that I delivered unto you*: so 1 *Cor.* 15. 3.

It is evident, *Act.* 1. 3. that Jesus Christ

Chrift fpake many things unto them betwixt his Refurrection and Afcenfion, concerning the Kingdom of God, *i. e.* efpecially the ftate of the Gofpel-Church, of all which we have no knowledge (I have not I am fure) in particular what they were, farther than is found in their precepts and practice, recorded in the New Teftament: And what if I fhould fay, that the change of the day from the laft in feven, to the firft in feven, was one of thefe things, I know not what could be faid againft it; but of that more hereafter.

7thly. Seventhly, Though I have declared, as above, my affent and confent concerning the Ten words to be perpetually obligatory, or a ftanding and unchangeable rule for all Chriftians in all ages to walk by, that fo they may walk in all well-pleafing unto God, (as once I heard very folidly proved by your felf, in an Exercife wholly upon that fubject, from *Pfal.* 19. 6, 7, 8, 9. as I remember) though I fay, and fay it again, that herein I confent with you; yet I fay it now, and muft fay it again hereafter, that the day of weekly holy Reft is altered, and yet
that

that alteration is no diſſolution of the Commandment, and that no tittle of the Law is broken thereby, and that the firſt day of the week is and ought to be as much the weekly Sabbath for the Chriſtians now, as the laſt day of the week was to the Jews of old; and that there is as good ground (though perhaps not ſo clear to every one) for the change of the day, as there was at firſt for the choice of the day: this is directly contrary to what you aſſerted in your paper.

I come now according as you deſired me, to take your 4th Propoſition in to conſideration, and your Reaſons in order as they ſtand, whereby you endeavour to confirm it, having again, and again in ſome weak meaſure, I praiſe the Lord, prayed for the aſſiſtance of the holy ſpirit of truth, to guide and direct me that I may write nothing againſt the truth, but for the truth; being at this preſent under the actual conſideration of the dreadful ſentence that I may be called to an account, I know not how ſoon, before the great and glorious God, for what I think, for what I write, as well as for what I ſpeak, or what I do: I bleſs God I am willing that truth ſhould be

truth

truth, and appear to be truth. Your fourth Propofition (though I have repeated it already, yet I think it meet to repeat it here again) is this;

The feventh day, which is the laft in day in every week in the weekly returns of it, &c. And for the proof of this, you produce *Exod.* 20. 8,9,10,11. *Deut.* 5. 12, 15. I conceive you lay the whole ftrefs of your Arguments upon that in *Exod.* and that you do not fo much as imagine, that *Deut.* the 5th affords you any more help, than what you have from the other alone.

This is that which is to be taken into ferious confiderations, whether your Propofitions takes in, or be agreeable unto the full fence of the Commandment, and that the Commandment fpeaks the fame thing that the Propofition doth; it feems as yet far otherwife to me, and that the Commandment requires only the obfervation of one day in feven, and doth not inftitute ny particular day, either the laft or the firft.

The laft of feven had its inftitution, as you feem to acknowledge, (which I was glad to find in your paper) in *Gen.* 2. 3. where, and when the firft day had its inftitution

tution will be enquired into when this Proposition is cleared, *viz.* That the fourth Commandment requires only the observation of one whole day in seven for the weekly Sabbath, not instituting either the first, or the last, for any such intent or purpose. And because, as *Solomon* saith *Prov.* 6. 23. that the Commandment is a Lamp, and the Law is a Light, I desire therefore in the strength of the Lord Jesus, depending upon him for light and direction, to look into the sence and meaning of this Law:

But first I shall premise this, That

As the second, so the fourth Commandment comes in some thing under a different consideration from most, if not from all the rest: my meaning is this; There is something in each of them is morral natural, and something which is only positive. In the second Commandment this is moral natural that God ought to be worshipped, not as men will themselves, but as God himself wills and prescribes; but in what ordinances, or acts of worship, this is only positive. So in the fourth Commandment this is moral natural, that there be a time, a sufficient time for the solemn worship of God, and yet such a sufficient time,

time, as leaves sufficiency of time for our worldly business and affairs. This the light of nature will teach, but without some revelation of the will of God, nature cannot determine the time, as to the frequency of its revolution, or if that, not the particular day that ought to be the time, which is the matter under debate betwixt us, but of this I shall have occasion to speak more hereafter: only I mention it here, because this is that which I have now to do, to give you my reasons why I conceive that what the substance of the fourth Commandment requires; either as naturally moral, or positively moral, or Gods manner of resting, or his blessing and sanctifying the day of his rest, or the revolution of time in which the day ought to be observed, whatever it be, reacheth no farther than the observation of one whole day in seven, not directly pointing out any particular day, but only by consequence at the last of seven because it was enjoyned before.

Now I cannot better nor in fewer words give you my reason of this, than to give you an account of my Faith, what I understand to be the sence and meaning of the Commandment, and it is this;

1. First,

1. First, I observe as it were the opening and giving forth of the Commandments, *verf.* 8. Remember the Sabbath day, that is, the day of holy rest of Gods appointing, to keep it holy to the Lord: In *Deut.* 5. 12. A text quoted in your paper, we have this which is the moral substance of the Commandment not given as in some other places it is, by it self alone, but together with all the ten words in its proper place and order; and which is to me very observable, the reason from Gods resting is omitted, neither is it at all enforced from the Creation, but from a Type of our Redemption, their deliverance from the *Egyptian* bondage. Such a material omission or alteration seemeth to be significant of something, whereof more hereafter.

2dly. Secondly, in the shutting up or Conclusion of the Commandment, *verse* 11. Wherefore the Lord blessed, and sanctified not the seventh day (of which more hereafter) but the Sabbath day of holy rest: this is evident, yet neither in the opening, nor shutting up of the Commandment where we have the moral substance of the Commandment, there is no mention on of any particular day at all.

3*dly*. I obferve what intervenes and comes in by way of explication or inforcement of obedience, between the opening, and fhutting up of the Commandment, and therefore incomes to be obferved.

1. Firft, In what revolution of time God had appointed this day of holy reft to be obferved, and that is one whole day of feven, of every feven days, fix for labour, one for reft, *verfe* 9. and former part of *ver.* 10. Thus far we have a comely order in the Commandment, fuitable to the infinite wifdom of God, firft fettling a day that ought to be obferved, and then the revolution of time in which that day ought to be obferved; how often, not one in twenty days, nor one in ten days, but one in feven days, one day in every week, which is well obferved by your felf in the third Reafon.

2*dly*. Secondly, I obferve the enforcement of obedience to the Commandment from Gods example of refting the feventh day, *verfe* 11. Here I do acknowledg the laft of feven is mentioned, but not as any branch of the unchangeable moral fubftance of the Commandment, nor the obfervation

on of it directly required but onely confequently, being inftituted before as is acknowledged by your felf: and it muft be acknowledged by all, that the laft of feven here mentioned, had firft of all the honor to be the day of Gods appointing, and accordingly it was obferved, and no other, till the time came that another day the firft of feven, was to fucceed in the room of it.

Thefe are the Particulars of the Commandment, which as far as I can apprehend, are moft obfervable in thofe four Verfes quoted in your Paper, and in none of them all can I find any thing that feems to give any Teftimony to the Truth of your Propofition.

1. Nothing as was faid before either in the giving forth, or fhutting up of the Commandment, there is no mention of any particular day, one or other.

2. Nothing in what intervenes between.

1. Nothing in what expreffeth the revolution of time wherein the day of holy reft is to be obferved. Six days fhalt thou labour, Thus I underftand this limitation, or rule for direction.

1. Six

1. Six days shalt thou labour, unless God otherwise appoint; and he did appoint in the old Administration, other days to be kept holy, which though not alway, yet sometimes fell out on some or other of the six working days. This I think none will deny.

2. Further, Six days shalt thou labour, not excluding the solemn worship of God out of those six days, as is well observed by your self: as if it were a sin for a man to hear a Sermon, or to set some hours apart for prayer any of these six days, as it is for a man to work upon that day of seven which God sets apart for himself.

3. And yet further, which is most to be taken notice of. Six daies, &c. rest one, not enjoyning the last of seven that was instituted before, but onely thus, Six parts of the time shall be for your selves, the seventh shall be mine, as *Gen.* 47. 14. you shall have four parts, saith *Joseph*, the fifth shall be *Pharaohs*. Let all be divided into five parts, four shall be for your selves, the fifth shall be for the King, not telling them which fifth but only one of five. So *Lev.* 23. 27. Let all be divided into ten, you shal have nine, the tenth shal be the Lords, not appointing

ing them which ten, but only one of ten. Thus I underſtand the word, ſix daies of the week ſhall be for your ſelves, one ſhall be mine. Thus I finde not one word for the laſt of ſeven, and which I muſt remember again, in the third Reaſon you plead the equity onely for one of ſeven.

I have heard that you alledged the Hebrew particle ה *verſe* 10. as emphatical; but becauſe you do not mention it in your paper, I ſhall ſay nothing to it now, but when you form your Argument from it, I ſhall give that which ſatisfies me for the preſent in Anſwer to it.

2. As nothing is here where the revolution of time is fixed which ſpeaks in behalf of your Propoſition, ſo I find nothing at all in Gods example for it; nothing there but one day of ſeven, from the beginning of the Creation; but it doth not therefore follow that it was the mind of God, that the ſame day muſt be obſerved for ever. I ſhall give you my reaſon why I conceive ſo, when firſt I have given you the ſence wherein I conceive the words are to be underſtood. Thus, We muſt not underſtand this properly according to the Letter, for the infinite glorious divine eſſence ceaſeth

no

no more to work than he ceaseth to be God; neither doth he rest as man doth, because he is weary, *Isa.* 40. 28. We are therefore to understand his ceasing to Create, from the works of providence ordering, and disposing all things that he hath made he never resteth, according to that *Joh.* 5. 17, Having thus given you the sence, now I shall give you my Reasons, why I conceive that this example of Gods resting is not alledged here to lay an obligation upon the Conscience, that the same day wherein he rested, which was the last of seven, ought to be observed for ever.

1. First, It seems to me to relate to what God himself did, rather then any way propounded as an argument to prove that for which you urge it. I will give you a parallel Scripture wherein the Example of the Lord Jesus is thus to be understood, 1 *Cor.* 11. 23. We have there the institution of the Lords Supper, when, and how it was instituted, repeated out of the Evangelists, and Chrifts example is related as to the time when, that it was not onely in the night, but in that particular night in which he was betrayed: now this is not recorded as a binding rule for our imitation, for then

night

night Administrations should not onely of absolute necessity be observed, but that particular night in which he was betrayed; which is commonly called with us Thursday night, which is more then ever I heard, that any one practised as a necessary duty; I am sure the Apostle *Paul* did not, *Acts* 20. 7. This example of Christ then, seems to be historically related, and whether the like may not be said of Gods example in the Commandments, let it be considered. But

2. Secondly, Though Gods example be historically related, yet it must be acknowledged to be ralated for some special end and purpose: As the example of Christ in the forementioned Scripture was without all doubt mentioned upon the highest ground of reason; which to speak of here thought it might be of good use, yet it would be a digression from the matter in hand.

And the special end, and purpose why Gods example is here related, seems to be this, even to shew that what is required in the Commandment is equal and reasonable, and for mans good: The holy Laws of God are often called Judgments, as for other

other Reasons, so specially I think for this, to shew that God requires nothing but what is just and equal. Thus God reasons the case with those, *Ezek.* 18. 25. *Hear ye me O house of Israel, are not my waies equal?* and therefore certainly the fence of the Argument from Gods example which doth best shew the equity of the Commandment, and to be for the good of those that observe it, is the best, and truest fence. Now to argue that because God wrought the six first daies of seven, and then rested the last of seven, this carries no convincing reason with it, that therefore we ought first to work six daies of the week, and then to rest the last day of the week, and to keep it holy to the Lord.

Reason, right Reason, if that alone were to judge, would rather judge it fit to keep the first of seven holy to the Lord, and seeing by Divine allowance we have six for one, take the six last to our selves. In reason we may hope, that the work on Earth will speed best, when our work for Heaven is done first: But now to argue from Gods example, that it bindeth neither to the first of seven, nor to the last of seven,

seven, but to one of seven, carries very great reason in it.

For if the great God, who needs not one moment either for rest, or for work, who never fainteth, who never is weary, wrought six dayes, and rested one, how much more should poor frail man, hold that proportion, who by reason both of bodily weakness, and spiritual wants, needs such a competency of time both for his worldly imployment, and Soul refreshments; and thus much you say your self hath been already noted. Thus you have my reason why I conceive there is nothing in Gods example, that affords any help to afford your Proposition.

3. Thirdly, I find as little in Gods blessing and sanctifying the Sabbath-day, for that which you alledge it.

1. First, To give the sence, [*he sanctified it*] *i. e.* separated it from common use, to be filled up with such duties as he appoints; and then [*blessed it*] *i. e.* appointed it to be a day of blessing. A day naturally considered, is capable of no other blessing, but only to be a means of blessing according to Divine appointment; but his blessing and sanctifying it,

secures

secures the blessing to the right observers of it.

Now for my reason why herein I dissent from you; 'tis this, He blessed and sanctified it, but not as it was the last day of seven, but as it was the day of his Rest, declaring thereby Creation work to be perfected. Neither was his resting, so far as I can see, the ground of his blessing and sanctifying it, but as considered in conjunction with the reason of his Rest, his finishing the Creation; and also with the result and consequence of his Rest, *viz.* his magnifying and honouring that day for the time being, above all other dayes, for the greatest work then in being.

Whether this blessing be applicable to no other day but this, as you say it is not, in the third Branch of the first Reason for the confirming your Proposition, shall be considered of when it comes to be spoken to, in order as it stands in your Paper; and I hope to make the contrary to appear, at least it appears so to me.

4. Fourthly, To mention it once again, though it was hinted before, in the very

con-

conclusion of the Commandment, *verf.* 11. though the laſt of ſeven is mentioned in the ſame verſe, in the words immediately foregoing, it is not ſaid, I mean in that place, that he bleſſed and ſanctified the ſeventh day, (though it be ſaid, that he did bleſs it, *Gen.* 2. in the ſence that is given above) but he bleſſed and ſanctified the Sabbath day. What ſhould be the reaſon of the ſudden change of the expreſſion? I conceive it may be this, and I think it may not be unworthy of your ſerious conſideration; it may be this I ſay, Becauſe the Command for the Sabbath day, was to be of a larger extent, than the laſt day of ſeven. I cannot but think, that if God had intended to bind his Church in all ages to the end of the world, to the laſt day of ſeven, as you conceive he hath done, he would have fixed upon that day in the concluſion of the Commandment.

Thus Sir, I have given you my reaſons why I diſſent from you, in that ſence which you give of the Commandment in your Propoſition: And why I adhere to that Propoſition, that the fourth Commandment requires only the obſervation of one

day

day in seven, not fixing it either upon the first, or the last day of seven, but only by consequence pointing at the last of seven, then to be observed, because it was instituted before, and to continue till the first of seven was to succeed it.

As *Solomon* said in the place formerly quoted, *Prov.* 6. so *David* his Father said before him, *Psal.* 19. 9. *The Commandment of the Lord is pure, enlightning the eyes;* and this is the light which the Father of lights hath given me from the Commandment. I shall shut up all that for the present I intend to say, as for the sence of the Commandment, with this; that as the second Commandment, as I said in the entrance into this discourse, may parallel with the fourth Commandment, in requiring something which is superadded to the law and light of nature; so 'tis evident in this, that as the second Commandment doth determine the worship of God, but only in the General, that it be according to his revealed will, and under that General, both old Ordinances, Sacrifice, Circumcision, and the Passover instituted, elsewhere are there required; So

Likewise New Testament Ordinances, Bap-

Baptifme and the Lords Supper are both comprehended, though neither named; fo in the fourth Commandment, both the laft of feven, and firft of feven, are comprehended, though neither of them directly named; but onely one of them confequentially as was faid before, becaufe formerly inftituted; fo that the fourth Commandment is perpetually obligatory for one day in feven, and then the fubftance of the Commandment is ftill unchangeable; thus the day admits of a change, not as a Ceremony, but as a Circumftance; the change of the day being no more prejudicial to the morality of the fourth Commandent, than the change of worfhip to the morality of the fecond Commandment.

And farther I add this, that I confefs I am at a very great lofs, how it fhould be fo as it hath been, and as it is at this day, that in a manner, the whole Chriftian world fhould centre in the obfervation of the firft day, if it had been a breach of the fourth Commandment which hath been fo often read, and fo often preached upon.

Before I proceed to fay any more than what hath been faid to thofe Reafons which

which are produced in your paper for the confirmation of your Propofition, I fhall give you in as few words as poffibly I can, what I have for the prefent to fay for the change of the day, from the laft of feven to the firft of feven; and that being done, I conceive I fhall not need to fay much to any of the Reafons, though I intend not, by the Lords affiftance, to pafs over any of them without faying fomething, and that as you defire, according to the order as they ftand.

To make entrance into this which I am now to fpeak unto; as none denies but that the laft of feven was the only day in the revolution of every week to be kept holy to the Lord to the end of the old world, *(i.e.)* of the Church that then was of the Jews, till the time of Reformation fhould come, *Heb.* 9. 10. fo I conceive it cannot with reafon be denied, but that fince the beginning of the new world, *(i.e.)* of the Chriftian Church, frequently in Scripture called the world to come, I mention only that *Heb.* 2. 5. fince then I fay, it cannot I think, with any fhew of reafon, be denied, that the firft of feven hath been generally acknowledged in all Chriftian Chur-

Churches unto this day, and will be (to speak as yet I do believe) till time shall be no more; though by what Authority, is the great matter in question, but the thing is certain, though it hath been of late, as I have heard, dropt up and down, in and about the Town, that this exalting of the first day of seven above the last of seven was done by the Authority of *Constantine*: I wondred at this when I heard of it, for though it be true that *Eusebius*, writing the life of that Christian Emperor saith, that by law he enacted, that the first day of the week, should be the great weekly holy day to the Lord: Yet to conclude from hence, that he was the Author of the change of the day; we may as well conclude that he was the Christian Religion; for by his publique Edict, the publique profession of it was established in all his Dominions, The Christians of those daies then receiving, as I have often thought, an answer to those Prayers which their Fore-fathers in Christianity no doubt poured forth before God, according to that injunction and direction, 1 *Tim.* 2. 1, 2. that they should pray for Kings and all that be in Authority, that they might lead a quiet and peaceable

able life in all Godliness and Honesty; which was much about 300. years before *Constantine* was born, at least before he sate in the Throne. Let *Eusebius* himself be consulted (I could easily quote the place if I had the book by me) and from him we may learn, that as the Christian Religion, so the Christian Sabbath was observed on the first day long before *Constantines* Cradle was made; and not only so, but before there was a Christian Magistrate in the world it was so: and yet, as 'tis apparent to me, by divine Authority, or else there was none in the world at all; for in the new world, that is, in the state of the Gospel-Church, old things were past away, old Sacrifices, old Covenant, old Sacrament, the Seals of the Covenant, this none denies; even so the likewise the old Sabbath: for the proof of this, let that Scripture, besides others that might be mentioned, be duly considered, *Gal.* 4. 10. The Apostle there reckoneth up several sorts of the Jewish Festivals, and condemneth the observation of them in all Christian Churches (for upon the same account he condemns them in one Church, he condemns them in all) This will appear to be

so

so, if we confider the Apoftles fcope in that, and in his Epiftles to fome other of the Churches. But to mention one is enough for all, it was to oppofe fuch of the Circumcifion as thofe mentioned, *Acts* 15 1,2. that mingled together the Law of *Mofes*, with the Doctrine of the Gofpel, and that in the matter of Juftification, and in order to Salvation; with this error, which was then a growing error, it is evident the Church of *Galatia* was infected, upon this account it might well be that he was Articled againft, for teaching every where to forfake the Law of *Mofes*, and againft the Temple, *Acts* 21. 28. as *Paul* himfelf no doubt knew that it was formerly an Article againft *Stephen*, that he fpake blafphemous words againft the Law, and that he fhould affirm that *Jefus* of *Nazareth* fhould deftroy the Temple, and change the Cuftomes that *Mofes* delivered them, *Acts* 6. 13, 14.

Object. If it be objected that the Apoftle there condemns their yearly Sabbaths, the Sabbath of the feventh year, the Sabbath of the fiftieth year, the year of *Jubile*, and not the weekly Sabbath.

By way of Anfwer, I defire that the words of the Apoftle may be duely weighed, ed; *Ye observe Dayes, and Months, and Times, and Years, I am afraid of you, left I have bestowed on you my labour in vain.* By Years, we understand their Yearly Sabbath, called the Sabbath of *Attonement*, and their Sabbatical years as above mentioned; by Seasons, their *Annual Feasts*, of the Passover, Penticost, and Tabernacles; and by Months, their Monthly Feasts called their *New Moons*, all this is clear; now I confess I cannot see what can possibly be meant by Dayes, but their weekly Sabbath dayes, especially finding in *Lev.* 23. where all their Feasts, and Holy dayes, eight in number, are reckoned up; their weekly Sabbath is put in the first place, as it were, by the Apostle.

I foresee two things may be objected against this Interpretation.

Object. First, it may be said, the Sabbath of the seventh day cannot be here mentioned, for then *Paul* should condemn his own Practice.

Answ. But this is easily Answered, for though we read, *Acts* 16. 13. that on the Sabbath day, that is I grant on the seventh day Sabbath, he went out of the City and preached to women, that resorted thither to
their

their publique worship: and *Acts* 17.2. that he preached in the Synagogue of *Thessalonica* 3 Sabbath days together, yet this was not as observing the seventh day Sabbath, but for the opportunity of the Jews assembling together on that day, which he could not have upon the first day; and so for a while condescending to their weakness, some other of the Jewish Rites, as may be instanced in Circumcision, were borne with. To conclude from hence that he did this as observing the seventh day Sabbath as they did, it may be well concluded that he did, and therefore we must observe the Feast Penticost; because he went up to *Jerusalem* at that Feast, as we read, *Acts* 18. 21. which we may be sure he did not for the Feasts sake, but for the Assemblies sake, that he might have the greater opportunity to preach the Gospel unto them.

But now if we would know what day of the week it was which he observed in obedience to to the fourth Commandment, look into his practice among the Converted Jews and Gentiles, and there we shall find that he observed the first day for the Sabbath day, and passed by the seventh day,

day, as will be seen by and by, in its proper place.

2. *Object.* It's objected by some, and those great and learned persons, that this Interpretation overthrows the Morality of the first day of the week, as well as the last day of the week, and for that end they thus interpret this place, and frequently urge it: But nothing they alledge from hence, I do acknowledge, could ever make any impression upon me, and my reason is this.

Answ. Look what those and the Circumcision, that were so zealous for the Law, sought to impose upon the Christian Churches, that and that only the Apostle opposeth: Now it seems to me beyond all question, that they never sought to impose the first day Sabbath, and therefore that stands, and will stand unshaken, notwithstanding this Interpretation of the Text; and the Interpretation standing firm, notwithstanding these Objections, it seems yet clear to me, that Christians are under no obligation at all to the old Sabbath, it is dead having served its time.

Quest. Now I know it will be asked,

if this be so, where have we any express institution either for the first day, or for any other day? Must we not then, if a word of institution cannot be produced, observe, as some say, every day for a Sabbath, or take that day those in Authority do appoint, be it one of 10, or one of 20, or have no Sabbath at all?

Answ. I Answer, Neither so, nor so, every day is not the Sabbath day, any more then every Supper is the Lords Supper, or every Table the Lords Table: Neither may we admit of one day of 10, or 20, for that is against the Morality of the fourth Commandment, which requires not only the observation of a Sabbath, but one day of seven for a Sabbath.

And that we have sufficient ground (which I confess can be no less than Divine Authority) for the first day of seven, I now come to give you my reasons why I so believe.

Only let me have leave first to ask, where is there an express word of institution for the last of seven?

In the fourth Commandment there is none, that only requires the observation

of

of one of seven; all the institution there is for it, is in *Gen.* 2. 3. which is not express, (though I acknowledge it sufficient) but only imply'd in those words, *God blessed the seventh day, and sanctified it*; and I hope there is as clear a word, (though perhaps not altogether found in one place) which implys the institution of the first day, as that which in *Gen.* 2. doth of the seventh day.

Before I proceed to that, I desire this may be observed; That there is the same reason for the institution of the first of seven, that there was for the institution of the last of seven. I said before what I thought to be true, that the Lord blessed and sanctified the seventh day; not only because he rested on the seventh day, having perfected the work of Creation; but also because of the result and consequence both of his rest, and of his perfecting his work, namely, his honouring and exalting that day above all other dayes; thereby now we know, that the memorial of those signal works of providence wrought upon the day, hath been the occasion of the advancing that day above other. So the Jewish Passover, *Lev.* 23. and the

Feast

Feaſt of *Purim*, *Eſt.* 9. 21, 23. and our 5th. of *November*, in memory of the diſcovery of that Treaſon plotted, and that nothing came to execution but the Traytors themſelves. Now this being acknowledged to be ſo, hence then it may be argued, That what day ſoever above all other dayes, God honours with his moſt eminent work, is to be the day of holy Reſt unto God. This will clearly carry it, and greatly ſtrengthen, though but an implyed inſtitution for the firſt day: for that was the day of the Lords reſt from the moſt great, and the moſt glorious of all his works, the work of Redemption.

I hear ſomething hath been alledged againſt this, that the firſt day of the week was not the day of Chriſts Reſurrection, and that the Tranſlators of the Bible have done us wrong in ſo rendring it: It is ſtrange to me if any ſhould ſay ſo, but I ſhall ſay nothing to it now, becauſe your Paper ſpeaks nothing of it; whenever you think fit to form the Argument from the error you ſuppoſe in the Tranſlation, there is as I underſtand one (and one that is well able to do it) prepared

to

to juſtifie the Tranſlation, and hath done it, many moneths ago; to him I leave it, becauſe, as I ſaid, your Paper gives me no occaſion to ſay any thing of it. However this I muſt ſay, for the proof of what hath been ſaid, I cannot but aſſert this, that it is an Article of my Faith, that the Lord Jeſus roſe again the third day, 1 *Cor.* 15. 4. *Luk.* 13. 32. *Mat.* 16. 21. and that as certain it is, that the firſt day of the week after his Paſſion week, is and was the third day after his Paſſion; the Lord of Life laid down his life, and was obedient unto death, the ſixth day of the foregoing week, which with us is called *Friday*, lay in the Grave the remaining part of that day, that night, and all the ſeventh day, (when the old Sabbath I think was buried with him) and then that night, and aroſe early the next morning, which was the firſt day of the week after his Paſſion; ſo that his bleſſed body continued in the Grave, two whole nights, one whole day, and ſome part of the two other dayes, the ſixth and the firſt of the week following, in all about 36 hours.

hours: And this was accounted three dayes and three nights, according to the allowed Dialect of that Nation, as one of the most learned in the Jewish Antiquities I think this Nation affordeth, by several instances makes good: And indeed there seems to be something in the Scripture for it, *Esthers* Fast was for three dayes, and three nights, yet on the third day after her Feast began, she presents her self before the King, and invites him to a Banquet, *Est.* 5. 1. This then is evident, the Resurrection of Christ, notwithstanding any thing that I think can be said against the Translation, was upon the first day of the week; besides what hath been said already, the Scripture is express for it, *Luk.* 24. 13. *The same day,* i. e. the day of Christs Resurrection, *the two disciples were travelling to Emaus*; and *vers.* 21. they say, *this day was the third day*: thus the Resurrection of Christ being upon the first day of the week, (though to speak properly it was not so much the ground, as the occasion of the choice of the day, because then it was manifested,
that

that the price of our Redemption was both paid and accepted) the day of Chrifts Paffion could not give the like occafion; becaufe though the price was paid, the Surety was not difcharged, the Grave was a part of his humiliation, he was not raifed from all the forrows of death, till he was raifed from the Grave, *Acts* 2. 24.

And as the day of Chrifts Paffion, could not for this caufe give this occafion for the change of the day, fo neither could the day of his Afcenfion. On that day indeed he entred into the place of Reft, to fit down on the right hand of the Father, but it was on the day of his Refurrection that he entred into the ftate of Reft; and this day, as I faid, on the firft day of the week, gives as fair and ftrong a ground, for fixing of the day of holy Reft, on the firft day of feven, as Gods refting from the work of the Creation did, for fixing it at firft upon the laft of feven.

If it be faid, by this means we blot out the memory of the Creation, which ought not to be done.

It

It is true, it ought not to be done, that marvelous great work comes within the compass of that Text, *Psalm* 111. 4. which ought to be had in remembrance, and the serious consideration of it, is a great relief in difficult cases: for what cannot he do that made Heaven and Earth of nothing? Thus they reason their hearts into a believing frame, *Psalm* 124. *ult.* that their hope, and their help, did stand in the name of the Lord that made Heaven and Earth: we ought therefore, as *Elihu* saith, to magnifie God in his works which men behold, *Job* 36. 24, 25. Only the work of Redemption ought more especially to be remembred, as the more glorious, and indeed the most glorious work: As therefore the work of Creation ought not to be forgotten, so the change of the day gives no cause for it; for as the first day of seven preserveth the memory of our Redemption, so one of seven preserveth the memory of our Creation, onely preeminence is given to the work of our Redemption. But it will still be enquired where is the word of Institution?

E

I Anfwer, 'tis acknowledged, that as I said before, I find no exprefs word for the Inftitution of the laft day of feven, fo we have no exprefs word in fo many letters, and words or fyllables for the Inftitution of the firft day of feven; but we have feveral particulars, which, not taken apart, but laid altogether, will clearly, and I think, undeniably imply it; and which was obferved in the fourth Propofition, which way foever God fpeaks his minde to us, we ought not to defpife him that fpeaks from Heaven.

Now among all thefe particulars, I defire thefe may be, in all fobriety and ferioufnefs, taken into confideration.

1. The firft is this, which I think none will deny; that Jefus Chrift the Mediator, had power to change the day: I do not, I dare not fay that he had power to change the moral fubftance of the Commandment, for it was not in his Commiffion; *He came not to destroy the Law, but to fulfil it*; not to change the day from one of feven, but

but that he had power to change from one day of seven, to another day: that Text which you quote three several times, sufficiently proves it; *He is Lord of the Sabbath*, (*i. e.*) of the day, and might do with his own what he pleaseth, even as he was Lord of the Vineyard, and might let it out to what Husbandmen he pleased, *Matth* 21. and that which we read, *John* 5. carries a probable appearance, that even then he began to manifest, that he had a purpose to change the day, for there we read, that having healed the poor diseased man who had been bedrid for thirty eight years together, he bids him take up his bed and walk; but why did he so? this was expresly against the letter of the Law; there was no necessity of it for the evidencing of the Miracle, that might have been done by his leaping, and walking; and the like was, *Acts* 3. and *Acts* 14. he might have gone home, and come again for his bed the next day; why then might it not be to shew that he had power and authority over that day, equal to what he had over the disease. To this purpose it is worthy our observation, that all along in that chapter, he juſtifies his Acts againſt the cavilling Jews, by aſſerting his power, as may be ſeen *verſe* 17. to the end of *verſe* 22. As it appears by this, that he had power to change the day, what, if it ſhould be ſaid, that he did according to his power actually change the day, though when, and how, it be not recorded. Let the fifth Propoſition be conſulted for this; there it appears, that there was word for inſtitution of Sacrifice, before *Abel* Sacrificed, (though it be not recorded when) becauſe God accepted his Sacrifice. So he hath accepted the Service upon the firſt day of the week, the firſt of ſeven, and bleſſed it as eminently he did the laſt of ſeven, as I ſhall ſhew when I come to ſpeak of your Reaſons. Why then might he not inſtitute this day, though it be not expreſs'd when, or where? What can be ſaid againſt it, but that he might do in the one as in the other? Though it be not recorded, why may it not be thought to be one of thoſe things which he had to ſay unto his Diſciples; and without he

did

did say to them afterwards, because they were not then able to bear them, *John* 16. 12. Surely the change of the Sabbath, which they with the whole body of that Nation, had such an high esteem of, would hardly then have been received by them.

4. Fourthly, To me it seems very evident, that the day was changed either by Chrifts own immediate appointment, or by his Apostles as they were guided, and directed by the holy spirit which they received, according to that promise, *John* 16. 13. and what they did teach, and practice as thus guided, and directed, ought to be received and believed, as if it had been immediately done by Christ himself, as was proved in the sixth Proposition.

5. Fifthly, and that the change of the day was thus appointed, either by Christ immediately, or by his Apostles as guided by the spirit of truth, these following particulars seem to me undeniably to prove it.

1. First,

1. First, by the Apostles practice let that be seriously considered, as it is recorded in several places. I shall begin with that, *Acts* 20. 7. it is there said, that when *Paul* came to *Troas*, where he abode seven dayes; upon the first day of the week, which is infallibly proved to be the day of Christs Resurrection, when the Disciples came together to break Bread, *Paul* Preached. I desire this Text may be considered in the fear of God. It was some grief to me to think how slightly, as I heard within these few daies, some turn it off: for if it be, as it ought to be, seriously considered of, it will appear to have much weight in it, for it is clear in the Text, that *Paul* continued there seven daies, and therefore was there on the seventh day Sabbath; yet there is no mention that either he, or the Church took any notice of it, more than of any other of the six dayes, but upon the first day, the work of the Sabbath was carried on, *Paul* both Preaching, and Administring the
Lords

Lords Supper. If this had been done upon the seventh day, and that he had begun his Journey upon the first day, it had made very much for the establishing of the old Sabbath; whereas now it makes much for the establishing of the new, and Christian Sabbath; if there had been but one such express Instance of *Pauls* Baptizing but one Infant in any of the Christian Churches, I think it would have prevailed much with those that are humble, conscientious, and godly (as I believe many are, that scruple much the Administration of that Ordinance to any that are not able to make profession of their Faith) if I say there had been but one such Instance, so plain and evident, in the Scripture; it would probably have prevailed much with them, though there are Arguments sufficient in the Scripture for it, yet they are not so plain to them: they would (it may charitably be supposed) have yielded that such an Apostle, would not have done this without Warrant, unless he had known the mind of Chrift for it yet you fee we have it for the Chriftian Sabbath, and fhall this fignifie nothing? Surely what ever it doth with others, it fignifies much with me.

2. Secondly, it is farther obferved, that the one hundred and twenty Difciples fpoken of *Acts* 1. and it may be fome more with them, met together diftinctly from the Jews, and did not keep the Feaft of Pentecoft with them, but together by themfelves; and this they did with one accord, as we read *Acts.* 2. 1. and this upon the firft day of the week, as may be undeniably demonftrated: The Lord Jefus was buried on the evening of the fixth day, that day being the firft in the Paffion week, but the feventh day Chrift refted in the grave, this was the fecond day in the Paffion week in which the firft fruit Sheafe of was waved before the Lord, *Levit.* 23. 11. and from this day they began to count their feven weeks to Pentecoft as in the fame Chapter verf. 15,

15, 16. (and which should be observed, this day *Christ rose again from the dead, and becomes the first fruits of them that sleep,* 1 *Cor.* 15. 20.) which being counted seven times, the 50th. day is just the first day of the week. So that it is clear, it was the first day of the week when the Disciples thus met together, to observe it in the duties of the day, which without doubt they knew to be the mind of Christ.

3. Thirdly, The Disciples met together twice on the two first dayes of the two first weeks, immediately after Christs Resurrection; if it be granted, that the first time they did not understand the change of the day, but shut the doors for fear of the Jews, because of the information of the Souldiers against them, that they had taken away the body of Jesus, what can be said against it, all things considered, but that they knew the change of the day at their second meeting? and that then they shut the doors for fear of the Jews,

Jews, because they did not observe the old Sabbath, the same that the Jews did, and as they themselves formerly had done. Thus much of the Apostles practice: Now it cannot be shewed, that ever they gave any respect to the seventh day Sabbath, as the day of holy rest unto the Lord, after Christs Resurrection; that of their Preaching sometimes on that day, was upon another account, as hath been proved already. Neither doth it appear that any other did, by what we find in the Scripture. Its true, those holy women mentioned in the Evangelists, observed it to the last, even to the day before Christs Resurrection, and it was their duty Christ being not risen. And for the Apostles, it is evident they shewed all respects after the Resurrection, to the first of seven, none to the last of seven: And further, it is not nothing what is recorded of the Lord Jesus himself, that he appeared so often unto his Disciples on that day: For though I lay not so much stress upon

upon it, as I have heard others have done, (for it is very probable, that during thefe 40 dayes, he appeared unto them upon other dayes as well as upon the firft day) but this I fay is not nothing, that there is no day mentioned by name, but the firft day; if it had been mentioned, that he had appeared unto them but once upon the feventh day, I cannot but think it would have been much infifted upon. Having now done with this, I proceed from the Apoftles practice to confider;

2. Secondly, Their expreffions; and that which I fhall here take fpecial notice of, is that in *Apoc.* 1. 10. where *John* gives this account of himfelf, that he was in the Spirit on the Lords day. This I have reafon to believe was the firft day of the week, and pointeth at the inftitution of it by Chrift himfelf; and my reafon is this, Scripture is to be interpreted by Scripture, even about the nature and meaning of a Phrafe,

unlefs

unless there be something in the Text where it is used, why it should not be taken in that Text as in others: This is generally acknowledged to be a good and safe rule for interpretation of difficult places; why then may not this Phrase prove it was the day instituted by the Authority of Jesus Christ, as being parallel with that of the Lords Supper, which was instituted by Christ himself? The holy Spirit of God directed both *Paul*, and *John*, in their expressions, neither of which is used but once a piece, and never applyed to any thing else in the New Testament, but to the Lords Supper, and to the Lords day; why should these Ordinances be held forth under the same expressions, if these had not the same institution?

It would seem strange to me, if any should say, that the Lords Passover in the Old Testament, (though a Supper Ordinance) was the Lords Supper in the New Testament; and it seems somewhat strange,

strange, if the seventh day Sabbath, which was indeed the Sabbath of the Lord under the Old Testament, should be asserted to be the Lords day in the New Testament, without some further proof than to say it is so: I could produce Testimonies from Antiquity, of some that lived near, and of one that lived some considerable time with *John* himself, who have interpreted the Lords day mentioned in the Revelation, to be the first day; but because you quote no such Testimonies, neither will I. I have been carefull to observe your order, and to proceed in this order onely in a Scriptural way: Thus much of the Apostles expressions.

From their practice and expressions, I come to the practice of the Primitive Churches, as they are recorded in the Scripture; as that of the Church of *Corinth*, 1 *Cor.* 16. 1, 2. and that of *Galatia*, and of *Troas* formerly mentioned, who had
their

their weekly Solemn Assemblies on the first day; I forbear to say any thing in justification of our Translation, because as I said before, you touch upon no such thing in your paper, desiring to be dealt withall in a Scriptural, not in a Grammatical way, only I cannot but add this, because I conceive it is according to Scripture, that it cannot with any reason be imagined, that these Churches would have made such an important change of the day for their solemn Assemblies, from what was formerly used by Gods appointment among the Jews, without consulting with some at least of the Apostles, and most likely with *Paul*, as being best acquainted with him. Hardly I think can there be produced any instance that particular Churches ever did determine any thing of this nature, by their own Authority, without consulting, I say, with some of the Apostles; considering how in other matters, not altogether of so great a concernment, they

con-

consulted with *Paul*, 2 *Cor*. 7. and as hardly can it be Imagined that the Apostles would ever give them any such direction, unless they had known the mind of Christ.

Thus, Sir, I have given you, in as few words as the matter would permit, a true account of the Reasons of my dissent from you, in the sense that you give of the fourth Commandment, and of what formerly hath and still doth satisfie my Conscience, that the day is changed, and that by divine Authority and that without any prejudice to the Authority of the fourth Commandment.

That which I have yet to do, is to give you my thoughts concerning your Reasons, produced for the confirming your Proposition, which may be done with a little addition to what hath been said already.

1. First, You say those weighty reasons which Jehovah the Saviour himself hath given, to enforce obedience

dience unto his Commandment, in observing a weekly Sabbath day holy to himself, do properly belong and are applicable to the seventh day, which is the last day in every week in order of time, in the weekly returns of it, as the weekly Sabbath day, and are applicable to no other day; and these you say are three.

1. First, You say, God rested only upon the seventh day, which is the last day in every week.

Answ. I answer, Thus far it is true, that God rested on the seventh day, the last day from the beginning of the Creation; but it seems to me rather as a reason of that limitation, six dayes of seven being allowed for labour, one of which seven was a day for holy rest, and not an argument engaging to observe the last of seven, for the weekly Sabbath to the end of the world: The reasons that prevail with me so to judge, I have given before.

2. Secondly,

2*dly.* Secondly, your second and third Reasons, I joyn them together, *he bleſt and ſanctified the ſeventh day*, becauſe you bring one and the ſame proof for both, and beſides they are to be looked upon in conjunction together, *he ſanctified the ſeventh day, by ſeparating it from common uſe, to be the day for his ſolemn Worſhip, and he bleſſed it, appointing it to be a day of bleſſing to the right obſervers of it.* In what ſenſe I underſtand this, I have given you an account before.

It is true, when this Law was firſt given to *Adam*, being then in the ſtate of innocency (ſo you acknowledge it was, and therein I aſſent and conſent with you) the bleſſing was applicable to no other day, but the laſt of ſeven; becauſe man continuing in that bleſſed ſtate, there was not, there could not be ſuppoſed a more eminent work than the Creation of the World; but now man being fallen, the work of Redemption being every way more glorious than the work of Creation, the bleſſing is applicable to the firſt day, the day of Chriſts Reſurrection, for then the work of Redemption was manifeſted to be fully perfected, and God bleſſed forevermore hath bleſſed that as eminently as ever he did the former day, not to mention that which

F   is

is and hath been done among the Churches of the *Gentiles*.

I desire you to look back to the second particular, and I think it is there made evident, that the Feast of *Pentecost* was on the first day, and then the Disciples being together, the Holy Ghost was given to the Disciples, then they received those miraculous gifts, and began *to speak with tongues*, which they never understood before, and *that day three thousand souls were added to the Church*, by the effectual working of the Spirit of God with the Ministry of the Apostles; and these Sermons they preached, that are upon record, after Christs Ascention: Was not then this day a day of blessing? was there ever a more eminent blessing, or any like unto it, on the old Sabbath, the last of seven? Whatever impression this makes upon the hearts of others I know not, for my own part I must needs say, I cannot but look upon it as very worthy of serious consideration.

2*dly*. Secondly, besides those Reasons in the Commandment you add further; 1. *The name and thing of a weekly Sabbath is given onely to the seventh day:* 2. *That no promise is made to the Observers of any other day, no threatning denounced against any that shall*

not

not observe any other day in the week, as a weekly Sabbath day, but onely the seventh, which is the last day.

A. To all these I answer from what hath been already said:

1. First as for the name and thing, this is that which I observe at first, and by this I am further confirmed in it, that you apprehend the last day of seven and the weekly Sabbath, *i. e. the day that is to be observed as a day of holy rest unto the Lord,* are Terms convertible; which to me is not yet proved, though I have considered your Paper from end to end, and I have given you my reasons why I yet believe, and must needs believe (till I see them answered) that another is instituted in the room thereof, and that by Divine Authority; so that though once they were, yet now they seem to me to be no longer Terms convertible.

2*dly.* Secondly, as to that which you say, *that there is no command for any other day,* I have already given you my sense of the Commandment, that no day is instituted there, first or last, nor so much as the observation of the seventh directly enjoyned there, but onely by consequence, because formerly instituted; so that both the Commandment and

F 2 th

the reasons of the Commandment reach the first of seven, as well as the last of seven: see before.

3dly. Thirdly, you say *there is no promise to the observation of any day, nor threatning against the not observing of any day as the weekly Sabbath, but onely the last of seven.*

A. I answer first, to speak properly (as I observe you do so) the promise is not made to the day, but to the right observers of it, in the duties that God appoints. Now the duties falling upon the first day of the week, as I have given you the reasons of my Faith therein already, the blessings annexed to the last of seven fall upon the first of seven, and have been given forth eminently upon the first of seven, as I have shewed.

2dly. Secondly, I answer farther, that as I find no blessing promised to the right use of the Seals of the Covenant under the old Administration, but what were then applied onely to the right use of Circumcision, and the Passeover; nor any thing against any Profaners or contemners of any Seals of the Covenant, but those that contemned Circumcision, and the Passeover; yet I am perswaded that you believe the Promises, I mean especially the Spiritual promises annexed to the old

Seals,

Seals, the right obſervers of the new Seals, Baptiſme and the Lords Supper, may in faith apply to themſelves. And the threatnings againſt the contemners of the old Seals, thoſe that contemn or profane the new Seals, have juſt cauſe to fear may fall upon them: even ſo the promiſe made to the old Sabbath the ſeventh day, and the threatnings againſt the tranſgreſſors of it, are applicable to the tranſgreſſors and the obſervers of the new Sabbath, the firſt of Seven; *whatever is written, is written for our learning*.

3*dly*. I now proceed to the 3*d* reaſon, which is this, *that God hath put this commandement for the laſt of ſeven into nature*; which if you had explained, as it ſeems you underſtand it, and that the Scriptures quoted had clearly proved it, I think I ſhould have been ſilent, and with a little more help I think ſhould have cloſed with you upon the whole in this matter. But I muſt crave leave to ſay, that to me your expreſſions are ſomewhat dark, and your proofs exceeding ſhort.

1. Firſt that your way of expreſſing your ſelf is ſomewhat dark: for you ſay, *God hath put this into nature*, but you do not expreſs what I do not clearly underſtand, whether you mean that is moral natural in the fourth Com-

Commandement, or which is moral positive.

2*dly.* Secondly, your Proofs, specially from *Rom.* 1. 20. *Psalm* 19. *Rom.* 10. 18. *John* 1. 9. seem to be intended for that which is moral natural, and there are some other Scriptures which to me have not the least appearance (pardon me if I say so) to be any thing at all to the purpose: and that there is one expression in your further inlarging upon this reason, which seems to be for that which is moral positive. For thus you say, *that natural reason will tell me, that seeing all men in all Nations do measure their time by weeks, and their weeks by seven dayes, that they should besides what they offer to God every day in every week, set apart a day unto their Maker, who hath allowed such a liberal portion unto them for themselves*: herein you will find, that I do both assent and consent unto you, when I have a little explained what I apprehend to be the difference between moral-natural, and moral positive laws.

1. First moral natural laws, I conceive to be these which the light of Nature, consisting in the knowledg of principles, and the law of Nature, in conclusions drawn from that light, acknowledgeth to be just and good, though they had never been written in the word. As

that

that there is a God, and *that this God is to be worshipped as God.* Thus much your proofs, especially that *Rom.* 1. 20. clearly prove, thus far the fourth Commandement is moral natural. The law and light of nature will teach men, *that there must be a time for the solemn worship of God a time of rest from all other imployments, a set time that must return according to some computation of time, either weeks, or moneths or years.* Let it be granted for *weeks* (though I would gladly see some farther proof for that, than yet I have seen,) this the nature of man even now corrupted, either doth acknowledg, or at least may be convinced of, by arguments drawn from these principles which are in the hearts of all men, when he is rationally urged with such principles as these, as *that all those things that are good, ought to be followed,* and *those things which are evil ought to be avoided* ; I mean such things, the goodness or evil whereof ariseth meerly from the things themselves, and may be acknowledged to be so, though the one had never been commanded, nor the other had never been forbidden in the Word. This is clear from that place you quote, *Rom.* 2. 14, 15. be pleased to consider the place, and I believe herein you will both assent and consent , that the Apostle

F 4   speaks

speaks of such things as the *Gentiles* without any revelation of the mind of God in his Word, had the knowledg of by the light of Nature, which they could never have of the last of seven for the weekly Sabbath, as will appear by and by.

2 *dly.* Secondly, Laws which are onely positive, I conceive to be such, as the light of Nature could never have judged either good or necessary, if they had not some way or other been revealed to be the will of God; the goodness of them arising onely from the will of God enjoyning them, who having absolute authority over all, may, and doth dispose of them into what condition he pleaseth, and imposeth upon them what Laws seem good in his sight; so that if they had never been enjoyned, the omission of them had been so far from being sin, that if any single person should have imposed them upon himself, or any number of men had imposed them upon others, as any part of Spiritual homage and worship which is due to God, it had been rejected as Willworship. Of this nature was the law given to *Adam*, of *not eating of the tree of knowledg of good and evil*; there was no evil in the fruit of the Tree, it was the creature of God, and all that he made *was very good*; it was onely

evil

evil, becaufe forbidden, fuch were the laws for facrifice, burnt-offerings, and peace-offerings, all the goodnefs that was in them was onely from the will of God appointing them; the light of Nature could never have feen the good of them, nor the law of Nature ingaged a man to the obfervation of them, if the will of God had not one way or other been revealed concerning them. The humane nature in *Adam* was created righteous, but if the revelation of the Will of God had not been fuperadded to that knowledg wherein he was created, he could never have known but that he might as lawfully have eaten of that Tree, as of any other. It is true, when the will of God was revealed to him, he had that written in his heart, by which he faw obedience to that Law to be both juft and neceffary.

Of this nature I conceive was the law concerning the laft day of feven, for the day of holy reft *to be obferved unto the Lord.* In the firft propofition I fhewed there is no goodnefs in one day more than another materially confidered, none in the laft of feven, none in the firft of feven; therefore neither of thefe were written in Nature: onely this is written in Nature, that when the will of God is revealed concerning any fuch pofitive law, as concerning

ning either the last of seven, or the first of seven, to be observed, even Nature as it is corrupted cannot deny but that it is both just and necessary to yeild obedience thereunto. Nature, corrupted Nature cannot deny, but that the will of the Soveraign Law-giver ought to be the rule of the Creature, and indeed I am apt to think this is all you intended to prove, and if no more, then I do declare herein both my assent and consent: but then this is far short of what the reason is brought to prove, namely that which is in the fourth Proposition, *that the last day of every week, in the weekly returns of it, is alone the particular day in every week, which is the weekly Sabbath day to be kept holy to Jehovah, in obedience to his Command as such.*

Let it be granted, which yet I confess I am not fully satisfied in, that the light of Nature without any revelation might have fixed upon one of seven, yet if God had not revealed his Will therein, it could never have fixed upon the last of seven; I think it would rather have fixed upon the first of seven for the reason alledged *pag.* 34. Surely, Sir, if the Law for the last of seven had been written in the heart of man, we might hope to have found it fairly written in the renewed and
sancti-

sanctified heart of the people of the Lords choice. But this the experience of all ages contradicteth. If any should speak to me in the language of *Eliphaz, Job.* 5. *Call now if there be any that will answer thee*; and to which of the Saints wilt thou turn thee and ask them, *Did you ever find this Law for the last of seven to be written in your heart?* they would for the generality of them tell me, *No, they never found any such matter.* This I believe would be the answer, or much to this purpose, even of those that were most holy and learned, most dead to the world and most alive to God, yea of the most faithful Martyrs of Christ for these sixteen hundred years, that with a good Conscience they could have done, as no doubt they did as there was occasion, any work of their Calling upon the last of seven, which upon the second, third, fourth, fifth, and sixth days was lawful and fit to be done, and that they never found any thing written in their hearts giving any check thereunto.

Either then the holy Law of God was not written in their hearts, which must not be admitted, or this Law for the last of seven was not written there as the rest were; which I really believe, and therefore give my dissent to this Reason. *4thly.*

4thly. Fourthly, there is yet one reason more must have something spoken to it, and that is *the example of the Lord Jesus*; and to this I say,

1. First, that his example is proposed to us for imitation, as those many Scriptures you quote do sufficiently prove: and herein I assent and consent with you; for though I dare not say with the *Socinians, that the grand end of Christs life and death was for example to be imitated,* (cursed be that opinion which presseth the *Imitation* of Christ to overthrow the *Satisfaction* of Christ) yet this I say with you, *that for our example he is proposed,* but yet with limitation, as not in his mediatory and meritorious work, so not in every occasional work, as his spending a whole night in prayer, nor in administring the Lords Supper at night; yet even in this, though we are under no obligation always to do so, yet when a just occasion serves it is lawful for us at least to do so. But that wherein his example is obligatory, is to imitate him in the exercise of those Graces, and practice of those Duties which belong to all Christians, *Mat.* 11. 29. *Coll.* 3. 13. 1 *Pet.* 2. 21, 22, 23. and such like. In all these, as he is by his Spirit dwelling in us the *principle* of holiness, so in his example

example he is our *pattern*; and indeed practical Christianity may be said especially to consist in walking as he hath walked, according to that you quote in 1 *Joh.* 2. 6. But now as to this particular for which you urge it, concerning the observation of the last day of seven,

1. First, it is granted, that notwithstanding all the *Jews* Cavils against him for transgressing against the Law, yet he perfectly (though not in their sense, as in all things else) fulfilled the righteousness thereof: I mention onely that one Text *Luk.* 4. 18.

2. Secondly, but this was during his state of Humiliation, being made under the Law, but (as I have said before) after his resurection I do not find that ever he took any notice of it, or shewed the least respect unto it during those forty days between his resurrection and ascention, though he both owned and honoured during that time the first day of the week.

3. Thirdly, the holy Apostles never imitated his example herein: I mean not after his resurrection: For though as I said whilst the *Jews* were any thing tractable, *Paul* especially took the advantage of the 7th day Sabbath to preach unto them, but with both converted

Jews

Jews and *Gentiles* he observed the first day of the week, as hath been shewed. So that for ought I find in your Paper, I conceive we are no more bound to imitate him therein, than in being Circumcised, or in deferring being baptized till we begin to be thirty years old, having no more Law for the one than for the other, and where *there is no Law, there is no Transgression.*

FINIS.

THere is lately published in *Latine* the so much expected Account of the late dreadful Plague, sold by *Joseph Nevil* at the *Greyhound* in St. *Paul's Church-yard*, Entituled, ΛΟΙΜΟΛΟΓΙΑ, *sive Pestis Nuperæ apud Populum* Londinensem *grassantis Narratio Historica. Authore* N. Hodges M. D. è *Collegio* Londin.

There is lately published
in Latine the fo much
expected Account of
the late dreadful Plague, fold
by *Joseph Nevil*, at the Greyhound in St. Paul's Church yard,
Entituled, ΛΟΙΜΟΛΟΓΙΑ,
five Pestis Nuperæ apud Populum
Londinensem graffantis Narratio Historica, Author N. Hodges
M. D. è Collegio Londin.

6. Band

Milton Keynes UK
Ingram Content Group UK Ltd.
UKHW022026071223
433887UK00007B/852